Brothers Four

Reliving the Great Depression and World War II

by

Jock Davis

DEDICATION

I would like to dedicate this book to my three
grandsons. All three of them are patriots,
serving our country in
AN ARMY OF ONE.

LT. COLONEL PHILLIP CAIN BAKER
MAJOR PATRICK JOSHUA BAKER
CAPTAIN JACOB ZACHARY BAKER

TABLE OF CONTENTS:

CREDIT TO THOSE WHO HELPED:

My sincere thanks to those who worked ardently to make this book a huge success. Those are:

EDITING:

Dr. Hilda Turner - Arkansas Tech University
   retired
Dr. Mary Ann Rollans - Arkansas Tech
   University
Mrs. Cherie Roe - Dedicated Friend

COVER OF BOOK ART WORK:

Mrs. Cain Baker, Washington, D.C. – Grand
   Daughter-In-Law; and Jeff Terry

SPECIAL TASKS AND ENCOURAGEMENT:
Many thanks to my good friend and mentor, Mr. Greg Sykes, author and pastor of First Baptist Church, Russellville, Arkansas for assisting with the publishing of this book.

To all of these fine people, I say THANK YOU very much.

PREFACE

"Moments are remembered more than days." I suppose that is the reason I have written this book. Growing up with three brothers during the depression and then facing separation and maybe death, with all of us in the service during WWII, made writing this book an easy task.

I remember times like when my father passed away when I was 13 years of age and exhausting every avenue in finding some means to serve a meal. Looking for work and finding it.

Reviewing past history of not only my immediate family, but my offspring, really gives me a yearning to live far beyond my years.

My mom, a widow with four boys to feed and clothe and get in school, gave the ultimate for us all. Some way, somehow, she always came up with a meal. In those days you did not ask if there was something better to eat, you were glad to consume what was in front of you.

Remembering this love that embraced all of us, it will never leave my body or mind. Gathering close to listen to the battery powered radio or to discuss the day's events after work and sharing any good news that was available, was the order of the day.

In all of these tough times, I never once heard my family complain. We were all happy to be healthy, to be together and pull as a team, which we did.

Sharing all four of our plights while in the military, after it was all over, is something that should be recorded. The many stories of my brother Ed's flights over Germany in his B-26 on bombing runs and his returning to base with the cables destroyed and landing safely was a miracle.

I remember listening to my brother, Roy, discuss his job as a drill sergeant at Texas A&M. He was the only brother who did not like the service. He joined the Marines and spent over three years detailing the lives of young people as they marched off to war.

Of course my baby brother, John, was in the Air Corps as a Pvt., was elevated to the rank of Sgt. and served overseas for quite some time.

Our dad, who had served in WWI, was wounded in the battle of the Argonne Forest. He then came back to Hope, Arkansas, met my mom, was married and they soon became the proud parents of four boys.

I like to remember the old saying, "Shave

and a haircut, two bits." Of course, "two bits" was a 25 cent piece. Oh yes, I remember the old hand-held clippers that would pull hair from your head when it would hang and the children would scream, "That hurts."

I remember stopping at a Filling Station, (service station), pumping up five gallons of gas in a glass cylinder, filling the car and going into the store to pay the owner 10 cents a gallon.

Walking to and from school was for everyone. Kids did not have cars in those days, so we walked about five miles a day to and from school in all types of weather.

I can even remember caddying for a banker who played golf every Sunday afternoon and he always picked me to caddy for him. There were no golf carts in those days, with walking as the only source of travel around the golf course. Oh yes, his bag was heavy, but just think, he paid me 50 cents per round! How well I can remember those little round greens that were indented about a foot downward and were filled with oiled sand to putt. After the putting, it was the job of the caddy to drag a door mat, with a bridle, around and around until all the footprints were removed. This is where I gained my love for golf.

There are so many things in my life that I have achieved and that I am so proud of. I have attained my private license in flight, received a college degree, and retired from the Army. I learned the game of golf and still enjoy playing. I played football and basketball in high school. I have been overseas several times. I have many more accomplishments, but, the two main things I wanted to do, and still may do, is drive a motorcycle and learn to play an electric organ.

Having our daughter, watching her grow up and be successful and delivering us three Christian men of valor is something I am truly proud of. To have the opportunity to influence their young lives and watch them grow into great leaders in our Military, is a thing to be very thankful for and I thank God for them and their families.

It has been very gratifying for me to remember my years of volunteer work that have brought me many friends and made me a person of super self-satisfaction. Today I still volunteer for various and sundry programs, such as, the cancer "Relay for Life", and the "Salute to Freedom Committee" that works with our military and military affairs.

Then there was the "Cherokee Dancers" dance team that another fellow (Gene Burris) and myself directed for fifteen years. To watch the growth of these young men and watch them go on to be lawyers, doctors, dentists, etc. is gratifying. This work was a work of nature because of our camping and Indian lore. Being of Cherokee/Welsh descent helped in this capacity. It still excites me today for one of these young men, many of them now grand-dads, who come up to me and remind me of what glorious days those were and of how Gene and I taught them commitment to life.

My last twenty-five years, professionally, I have been fortunate to conduct my own seminars for graduating seniors at Land Grant colleges in Poultry Science. One of my favorite universities is Mississippi State University. This jaunt started over thirty-five years ago when I was recruiting students for management positions in our poultry company.

While working with this poultry company, in a personnel position, a friend and I came up with the idea of a seminar called GYST. I wrote my own handbooks and created learning devices and this spread throughout our company and finally to colleges that wanted to use it.

In teaching the GYST course, it has been so heartwarming to see young men rise from management trainees to six-figure salary executives.

Personal counseling as well as instruction has led to a new field in college preparation for graduation. To watch these young people set and reach goals was a thing of beauty.

There have been so many things in my life that have left memories of grandeur that I could not name them all. I could attest to the fact that to serve others is the most satisfying thing we could do in our lives.

As you read this book, please reflect back on your life as a young person and the travels you have made in life. It is my hope that you can take away from this writing something that will be beneficial in your future.

The only other thing that I would recommend to you is that you go to paper with your thoughts and ideas, and by writing your memoirs, recollect happy, as well as sad times in your life. It is extremely interesting to reflect on your past and remember things that have long been forgotten but that your family or others might enjoy reading. AND DON'T FORGET: "To expect more is to get more."

FOREWORD

In writing this book I have been challenged through memory to bring to the readers a real life story of a typical family during World War II. I have been surprised that my memory could take me back so many years, nearly seventy in fact, to bring happenings in my family's life to mind that all of you can relate to.

I do not want to infringe upon the wonderful book, "*The Greatest Generation*," written by the famous Tom Brokaw, but to bring you anecdotes of persons who actually endured this confrontation.

My love for my three departed brothers played a large part in writing "Brothers Four." I want the readers to actually see and feel the love, devotion and patriotism we all felt for each other.

I do wish to commend Mr. Brokaw on his writing of "*The Greatest Generation*." It was well-written but also needed, I felt, a personal touch by someone who had actually grown up during the depression and served his country, leaving behind a loving mother, who witnessed all of her boys serving their country.

Even though I am one of a few who lived to share with you the turmoil, love, gratitude and self esteem that came out of this conflict, I will try to the best of my ability to parlay my feelings and thoughts about those years of enrichment.

At the age of eighty-six, I have seen all of my immediate family go on to be with our Savior. Continuing to tell this story brings back many memories of which I am thankful for. My gratitude to my wife for being so patient while I struggled at the computer and my apologies to my golf buddies as I continue to write this book.

In honesty and humbleness I will try to deli-

Four brothers that loved each other very much

ver to you, the reader, a true assessment of my life and those lives that are mentioned. I will try to portray life as it was during the War and how it has changed so drastically today. Maybe my reflection on my past life will move you to do the same with your memories.

*****

There have been moments that I should have scratched the book, gone to play a round of golf, then done some gardening. But, I stuck with it and am so proud that I did.

We, the Davis Clan, were proud people. Though poor, we were always clean, dressed as nice as possible and always had good friends surrounding us.

I hope you will feel the inner feelings of my mom, as she wet her pillow with tears as she laid her head down to sleep, not knowing if any of her four sons would return from this war. With the radio as the only source of communications during the war, there was always a dread of that soldier, a stranger, stepping up on the front porch, hastening her to the door to say, "It is my duty to inform you..." Fortunately this was not the case, for all of us came home without a scratch physically, but, maybe affected to a degree, mentally.

I have either witnessed personally or through the service of my brothers, son-in-law, and grandsons, the wars and conflicts of WWII, the Korean conflict, Vietnam, Desert Storm, Enduring Freedom of Iraq and Afghanistan.

As our Bible states, "There will be wars and rumors of wars" before the end time. As the saying goes, "We ain't seen nothing yet."

I am concerned about our children and grandchildren. There is no telling what they might have to endure before their lives are over

I hope you enjoy this writing and Godspeed in all of your endeavors.

Major Jock Davis, proud to have served

PART 1

THE GREAT DEPRESSION

CHAPTER 1

DEPRESSION MEMORIES

There are so many vivid memories of those days of the 1920's, 30's and 40's. There was little money to spend. Food was scarce, there were few medicines that would heal the sick, and we had black and white movies, but there was much more love and harmony within the family than there is today.

You remember times when your mom wrapped your big toe, with it bleeding, with a piece of worn out sheet. Of course there was Mercurochrome, to put on it to kill the germs. But, who thought about germs in those days? Who even thought about death, sickness, let alone dying? Too much was at stake keeping kids in school, keeping them clothed, fed and somehow affording books for them.

Back in those days no one spoke of Civil Rights but I had a stern warning from my mom, saying, "You are not to play with the black children."

The black neighborhood included their housing, schools, football and basketball teams and their own events center. They all lived to themselves and never bothered our neighborhood.

I will never forget, being six or seven years old and my buddy and I would go to Garland Creek, a muddy little stream, not too far from town. We would take off our clothes and go swimming. It did not matter that there were water moccasins swimming with us or not.

One day we were swimming and two black kids came up, whom we knew, and we asked them to swim with us. Well, without any hesitation, these young men pulled off their short pants and hit the water. We had a ball that afternoon playing with these guys, dodging moccasin snakes and turtles.

Well, about two weeks later my mom asked me about the incident and I admitted that we did swim with the blacks. Mom said, "Jock, you know our rules, don't you?" I replied, "Yes, I do." She immediately sent me after a peach tree switch and she whipped me, and my crying was heard all over the neighborhood. Well, I can tell you that I did not disobey from that day forward.

Since there was no money to buy recreation you either made it up, built it yourself or you had nothing. On those hot days of summer when chores were done, one of my brothers would say to the other, "Let's roll some hoops!" To build a "hoop roller" you would take a small, straight board, about 2 inches in width and about 26 inches long. You would flatten a *Prince Albert* tobacco can and then bend it in the middle to have a trough effect. You would nail the can on the end of the stick and then you would be ready to roll the hoop. You would find a stiff, metal hoop that was round as possible, place the hoop on the ground with the hoop standing upright and start the hoop rolling forward. Going downhill, the hoop would really get to rolling and if you had a hard surface, like pavement, you could really move.

It was always a lot of fun for several of us to get together and map out a route around town to roll our hoops. There were times that I know we would push our hoops for at least five miles.

Now with all of this said, most people would say, "What a waste of time." To the contrary, though, this kept us out of trouble, kept us out from under Mom's feet and we learned a bit about motion and carpentry. And it was a great lot of fun!

Another thing we would do was "walk the tracks." Have you ever tried to walk railroad tracks, barefoot, on a hot summer day, just to see how long you could stay on? I want to tell you that you can't walk very far before jumping off of the tracks because they would be so hot.

I had a good friend and he and I would walk several miles to see who could walk the farthest, with shoes of course. One day, someone mentioned to us that we could walk farther if we held hands while walking on the tracks. We tried it and sure enough we did get quite a distance. Again, this a very time consuming pastime but it was a lot of fun!

After the corn harvest in the fall, everyone had their barns full of corncobs. A neat game that we played was about six of us boys would choose sides. We would soak a half of a cob in water overnight. We would put them in a sack and then the
fight was on. Oh yes, we had knots on our heads and some bruises but it was so much fun to make your best throw and paste the guy on the other side and hear him scream.

A game that we truly loved was to take a rubber ball and play "Annie Over." Two of us would get on one side of the house and two on the other side. One side would yell "ANNIE," and the other side would reply "OVER," and then let the ball fly over the house. You would have to catch it before it hit the ground. This was probably the most fun of all of our self-made games.

I also recall very well my buddies and I mocking Tarzan by climbing to the top of a large sycamore tree and swinging from limb to limb with the famous Tarzan call coming forth. None of us were ever hurt, but, now that I am retired, I think about what would have happened if we had been twenty or thirty feet in the air, jumped to catch a limb, and it be rotten? We would have hit the ground and been killed.

During the depression years, all of the kids in our town went barefoot during the summer.

You had to dodge the "mad" dogs in the neighborhood for if you were bitten you would have to take a series of rabies shots in your stomach. We stayed away from the dogs.

If my memory serves me right, the only medicine that was of benefit were Sulfa Drugs. Penicillin came along at the close of WWII and Sulfa was the drug of choice. Of course there were vaccinations for various and sundry diseases but people did not have the money to spend on vaccinations, they were too focused on putting food on the table.

My mother felt very strongly about seeing that all four of we boys were in Sunday School on Sunday morning. I will never forget my aunt making me a suit out of CCC OD material. I was so embarrassed to wear that suit to Sunday School and I can well remember that I was never made to wear it again.

At the age of twelve, when school was out and the grass had begun to grow, my dad took me by the hand and said, "Jock, you must make your own money for school clothes and shoes, so I am taking you to the Western Auto store to buy you a lawn mower."

"Well," I thought, "this is OK." Until my dad said to the man selling the mower, "My son is going to make his school money by mowing yards. He will pay you a dollar per week until the mower is paid out." With this statement, dad pulled out a dollar for a down payment and I was to pay the other nine dollars out of my earnings.

Those of you who are old enough to remember will recognize what a reel type mower is. It did a good job on small grass, with the exception of the tall individual weeds that grew up in the midst of the short grass. The homeowners began to chastise me for not cutting the tall grass, so, I went back to Western Auto, charged the amount of a "sling blade," and went back and cut the tall weeds down.

The normal rate of pay for mowing a yard of at least a quarter of an acre was fifty cents. If you worked real hard five days a week, you could make four or five dollars per week. Well, I worked hard at getting people to let me cut their yards and at the end of summer I had enough money to buy all of my khakis, one pair of shoes and my books for school.

As time went on, I found, as did my other brothers, that everyone in the family would contribute some way or another. My dad was a debit insurance salesman, owned a model A Ford sedan and made a modest living for his family. My mom never worked outside the home, for in those days, other than waitress work, there was little work to be had.

One thing I can remember was that when our family sat down to a meal, my dad would always bless the food and we never complained about what was on the table. Another thing we always did was clean up our plate. There never was any food left to be thrown out.

My dad was a generous man. In those days, there were tramps who rode trains from town to town looking for a handout, a meaningful job or something to eat. There would come a knock at the back door when we would be getting ready to eat and my dad would say. "Cecile, set another plate, we have company."

Dad would invite the dirty tramp into our home, show him where to wash up and he would break bread with us. Of course we boys would love it because this person would share his travels with us which was unbelievable. Many of the places they would mention, we had never heard of.

My dad was of the Baptist faith and the rest of us were Presbyterians. I just wonder today what dad would think about old Jock being a Baptist?

In those days the best you could do for music was a battery powered radio. They sounded good but there were few radio stations. A memory of the Joe Louis fight lingers in my mind.

There are so many instances where my memories as a child are so vivid it is unbelievable.

I had a good buddy, Alvin Reese, who was my age and lived across the street from us. He also was about 10 or 11 years old. Alvin and I spent many hours during the summer months dreaming up ideas of things we could do to stay busy. For instance: One fall afternoon we decided to gather pecans out of our yard, place them in quart fruit jars and sell them. Well, that wasn't successful at all because no one had money to buy them. Alvin and I had heard that there was a circus in town about a mile from our houses. We gathered 2 quarts of pecans, each, and headed for the circus to try to use them in some manner to enter the circus.

We found a hired hand driving stakes around a tent and we asked him what he would be willing to do for a quart of pecans. He said, "I will slip you boys in under the tent to the Hoochie Coochie show."

We both agreed, gave him the pecans and he slipped us under the tent. Lo and behold there were hula dancers, half naked, dancing on the stage. Man, did we get an eye full. We couldn't wait to get to some of our friends and explain in detail what the show was like. Our mom never knew of this outing.

Then there were the gypsy groups who traveled the countryside. They would set up tents, make music, cook outside and then move on to another area. We heard that they kidnapped kids and took them with them, therefore, we never visited their campsites.

When we were eleven years old, we joined the Boy Scouts of America. Camping was the big thing. One pretty spring day, Alvin and I asked our parents if we could go camping and we told them where we wanted to go. On this campout, we had planned that we would ride our bikes, such as they were, about 4 miles to a pretty creek and set up our lean-to. We would then let out our lines to catch some fish and cook them for supper.

We had each made a trailer for our bike. We used an apple crate and attached two wagon wheels to the back of the box and added a tongue that was to be attached to our bikes. We loaded our food and cookware in them and we were off to the creek.

After setting up our lean-to, we set out bank poles with our line and hooks attached, baited them, and by that time it was getting dark. We went back to the campsite, made a huge fire in front of our lean-to and began frying some Irish potatoes, bacon, eggs and bread.

Well, about an hour later a large spring storm began to gather and lightning started flashing. We were scared to within an inch of our lives.

The wind began to blow and buckets of rain fell. We crawled as far back in the lean-to as we could and we, and all of our belongings, stayed completely dry. We slept well after the storm passed.

The next morning we began to "run" our fishing lines and every one of them had a pretty good sized fish on the hook. On one of them was a three pound bass and the rest were catfish. Alvin and I dressed the fish, wrapped them good, packed our trailers and left for home.

Upon arriving home, our families were sure glad to see their eleven year old boys and hear their many stories about their encampment and the big storm.

*****

I suppose one of the most hated jobs that mother had given me to do when I was young was to dig the Bermuda grass out of her garden in the spring, in preparation for planting later on. The minute I would get home from school she would direct me to the hoe and I knew what that meant. Of course, later on, I was glad to enjoy the green onions, radishes, lettuce and the likes, that she would serve us for supper.

There are many things that I regret, as a kid, that I would do that wasn't really bad, but today I would not think of doing them.

I remember one balmy August evening, my mom and I and two of my aunts were sitting out on the porch enjoying what air there was available. There was no air conditioning in those days and because of the cost, you rarely ran the electric fans.

My buddy came by and gave me the idea of scaring the black folks who were walking home from town. That night was very dark. I rummaged around until I found a pair of my mom's black hose and we stuffed them with rags, and then tied
one end of the hose to a long string. We then got behind some bushes so the blacks could not see us, and pulled the hose, like
a snake, in front of the walking black people.

Well, those ladies jumped three feet into the air and yelled loudly, "Oh Lordy, there is a snake." And they took off running as hard as they could run. After the commotion died down, mom came to the side of the house and heard my buddy and me laughing and, then again, the switch came into play.

In the summer time we were always looking

for something to do. If it wasn't making rubber guns, or bean shooters, we were digging caves or tunnels under the ground. This was real work, but we enjoyed doing it and having fun.

I can well remember my first try at chewing tobacco. I was fifteen years old and was playing basketball. I had just put on my uniform and was shooting long shots in the gym. I had another good buddy who was shooting with me. He came up to me and said, "Jock, have you ever chewed any *Days Work* chewing tobacco?" I said, "No, I haven't but I have seen guys cutting off some with a knife and it sure does smell good."

He cut off a pretty good sized chunk and offered it to me. I threw it into my mouth and continued to shoot around the goal. I went up for a jump shot and came down too solidly and that wad of tobacco went to the bottom of my stomach.

Well, I can tell you that I have never been so sick in my life. I left the court, went to the dressing room, got on my knees by the commode and emptied my stomach. I got dressed, went home and never chewed tobacco again.

When I was fifteen years of age I was lucky

to get a job at a stave mill outside of town. I believe the job paid fifty cents per hour for eight hours of work. This was in the summer time and I needed the money to pay for clothes and books and to help my mom.

The job was simple but time consuming and hot. I would stand at the end of the line where the turn knife would go in a circular motion, around the stave. It would slice a quarter of an inch thick slab that was three feet long and eighteen inches wide. It was my job to catch the slab, place small sticks between them and stack them in a pile three feet tall.

In the mornings, a pick-up truck would pick us workers up and we would pile in the back of the pick-up and be transported to work.

Well, there was a black fellow, about middle-aged, who rode with us and the fellow who owned the truck had a large cur dog that rode in the back with us as well. I had noticed that the black fellow, about halfway to work, had gotten real nervous.

As we went along, the dog was facing the road, looking at the vehicles following us and wagging his tail. I did not know it at the time but the wagging of the tail was irritating to the black fellow. All of a sudden, he picked the dog up and threw it out of the back of the truck while we were doing about thirty five miles per hour.

I asked him why he did that and he remarked, "I cannot stand to see that dog waggin it's tail toward me." When we arrived at the stave mill, there was no dog to be seen. The owner asked about him but none of us opened our mouths and that was the last I heard of the missing dog.

*****

Since food was hard to come by, especially meat, hunting and killing your own food was the thing to do. Somehow we were able to buy a box of twenty gauge shells to go rabbit hunting. At that time no one knew of blood poisoning through eating wild animals.

When winter time came, my brothers and I would go hunting. We had a small beagle dog and he was good at chasing rabbits right past us and one of us would get a good shot. Well, since I was the youngest of the three, I was not allowed to shoot and had to stand behind the other two and watch them shoot. It was nothing out of the ordinary to kill five or six rabbits in one day.

Our dog would jump the rabbits out of a stack of stubble in a grain field and run them right by the shooter. In those days there was no game and fish commission, so there was no limit. We would kill what we would want to clean and cut up and that was it for a week.

Mom would soak them overnight in salt water, the next day she would drain the water off, salt them, cover them in flour and fry them in pork lard.

Today we would not think of using lard to fry them in, but in that day, lard was very tasty and enhanced the taste of the rabbit. Mom would make a large bowl of flour gravy, bake a pan or two of biscuits and boy was that a meal.

Another high time was that of hog killing. Dad would feed a hog all summer and when the hog was two or three hundred pounds and the temperature was 32 degrees Fahrenheit or below, he would kill the hog, scald him in really hot water, scrape the hair off him, remove the entrails and cut the critter up in pieces.

Normally the best way to handle the hog was to use the hams and shoulders as "hanging meat" in the smoke house and cut up the rest of the pig to fry, bake or cook in some way. Normally the hams and shoulders were sugar-cured before they were hung and smoked in the smoke house. My favorite of all of this killing process was the process of making "cracklins."

You would take the hog's skin with about an inch or two of back fat attached, cut it up into squares about two inches long and drop them into a wash pot. You would cook them until they rose to the top of the grease, dip them out to drain on some type of cloth that would remove most of the excess grease, can them in a fruit jar, tighten the lids and you could enjoy them in "crackling" bread or just sit down and eat a few. I notice in the grocery stores that they are now referred to as "pork skins."

Oh yes, we made it through tough times eating things that you would not dare eat today, but we are none the worse for wear. I reiterate, there was no money, no food, no clothing and you did well to have some kind of frame over your head.

You know, we never grumbled if mom served us a supper that was hot cornbread, real creamery butter, molasses and a glass of milk. We were very fortunate to have meat of some sort on Sundays.

I remember well this fellow driving a T-Model Ford pick-up with a screen wire rack over the back. Hanging in the back from the top of the rack were sides of beef. Normally he never came around in the late summer because of flies and spoilage of the meat.

I remember he would pull up to the front of the house and honk his horn. Mom would go out and pick out a beef roast. He would then cut it off, wrap it in an oily looking piece of white paper, tie it with a string, and she would pay him and into the house she would go.

You might ask, what was the refrigeration like in the depression days? Well, it was very simple. Along about this time, the wooden ice box became an item that everyone wanted. We had the good fortune of buying a used one.

We had a wooden ice box that was lined with metal, with a hole in the top that would hold ice, and of course, a drain. You were supplied with a pound card to place in your front window which would indicate if that day you wanted 5, 10, 25 or 50 pounds, with that number of the card turned top up. The ice man drove a one-horse wagon that had 500 pounds of block ice on the wagon.

If you wanted 10 pounds, he would chip off an estimated ten pounds, place it on his leather-covered shoulder with ice hooks, enter the back door and place the block in the top of the ice box. The ice man hardly had to say "Whoa" because the horse knew the houses that usually received ice.

There were no frozen products at that time. You either had ice or you had no refrigeration. I was eighteen years of age when I first knew of frozen products. There was a tugboat with frozen rabbit on board being delivered from Australia to us in New Guinea during WWII.

Jock, age 5

CHAPTER 2

FAMILY EARLY ON

My dad was raised in Peoria, Ill. He entered WWI and served overseas and battled in the Argonne Forest. When he was released from the service, he heard of an opening at a cotton oil mill in Hope, Arkansas. He applied for the job and got it.

My mother was raised in Rosston, Ar. Sometime that summer, my dad was watching a baseball game in Rosston and met my mother. They dated for about a year and were married.

My mother had never been out of Rosston, so dad, while dating her, decided that he wanted to take her to Prescott, the county seat, and buy her a fountain coke. She had never had a coke and when she started drinking through the straw the fumes from the carbonation entered her nostrils and she thought she had been poisoned.

Those were wonderful years, even though it was right in the middle of the depression. My dad was an insurance salesman, a good one, and he drove a Model A Ford Coupe. As a debit salesman, he would sell a policy and collect for it also. He would even take food stuffs for money. Somehow he would get the money and send it in to the company. Many times we would have bacon, hams, eggs, and other items to eat that we would otherwise not have.

There were four of us boys; Roy C., the eldest, Edward W., and then next in line, me, "Jock." My baby brother, John Edsel, came along about five years after my birth. The three of us babied him, of course, and wouldn't let him follow us on hikes, etc.

Being the third boy in a family of four boys wasn't easy growing up. First of all my two older brothers, Roy and Ed, were so close, I was in the middle and secondly, my baby brother, John, because he was "the baby," was really taken care of.

I was born in 1924 so you can draw your own conclusions on how old each of us were.

It was tough clothing four boys and feeding them.

I had an uncle, Uncle Willie, who lived down in the country, near Prescott. The place was called Cale, a small town about sixteen miles from Prescott, which was a long way in those days when you consider that my dad drove an A Model Ford for his work. Uncle Willie worked at a saw mill and walked about four miles to and from work.

His pay was fifty cents per hour. I recall, as a six-year-old visiting he and Aunt Hop one summer, that he and I walked to the General Store and he traded enough eggs to buy me a pair of overalls. Man, was I proud of those overalls.

My early days during the depression were ones of happiness. We had no money to buy fun with, so we made our fun. For example, to paint thread spools with red juice out of a berry was a lot of fun. Of course, the soaps, not the quality we have today, did not readily take the color off of your hands, therefore you wore it off.

And there was the case of a bicycle to be used between the four boys. This bicycle was not new. My two older brothers, upon finding the frame at a junk yard, commenced to piece the bike together. They found forks for the front wheel to fit into, and rims to put spokes in and finally, they found tires which at that time were inflated with tubes with air in them.

There were no fenders that some have today and during a rainy day mom would have a tough time washing our clothes with mud down the back.

The big thing was to find some rusty nails,

find suitable old boards out of a barn, saw them into correct lengths and nail it all together to make a ladder. What a ladder. It was not very safe and was very heavy.

I recall that one day, at the tender age of six, mom asked me to check on the dried apples that were drying on a sheet that was spread on top of an old chicken house. The roof was rusty and rough.

Anyway, I made my way, carrying my heavy ladder to the chicken house and started my crawl to the top of the chicken house to check the apples. Well, right at the break of the roof, it seemed at the time that a thousand wasps had built a nest underneath the overhang.

About the time I reached this height, about five or ten of these huge wasps lit on my head and face and began to sting. I was too high to jump so I hurriedly crawled down the ladder screaming at the top of my voice for momma. Here came momma asking, "What is wrong Jock?" As I stroked my face and head I shouted, "Waspers."

She immediately removed a wad of snuff from her mouth and massaged every sting. There was some swelling but the snuff must have done the job.

My memories still linger of my brothers always coming up with some idea that eventually would get me in trouble. For instance, my older brother, Roy, decided that he was going to make a trolley by attaching a cable high in one tree and attach the other end to another tree approximately 100 feet apart. Then he would grease the cable with some of Momma's lard, place a short piece of pipe on the cable to hold onto, and then you were off to the bottom.

Well, Roy and Ed were heavy enough to make the pipe slide down the cable. They invited me to try it. I climbed up the nail-driven stakes on the side of the tree, grabbed the pipe but did not push off. It seemed like I must have been 200 feet in the air when really I was only about 25 or 30 feet.

Due to their coaxing, I pushed off, and with little weight on my body, there I hung about 20 feet from the ground. I must tell you, I was scared to death. They began to yell, "Let go and we will catch you." The louder they yelled, the more I cried.

Finally, at their coaxing and due to tiring, I let go and they did catch me before I hit the ground. I never did try the trolley again. Of course I had mom's ear and would run to her screaming, claiming that my older brothers were mistreating me. She would usually soothe me with a cookie and have me ready to give my older brothers another try.

Time came when I had to enter the first grade at the age of six years. I did not want to go to school but dad finally said, "Jock, you are going to go." So, with my lunch bucket, I started off to school. When the bell rang, I decided I would go home, I was homesick. So one of my brothers came home immediately and we walked back to school. My dad finally told me that he was going to send me to an orphanage if I did not stay in school.

One morning Roy asked me to go along in the A-Model and throw the Gazette for him while he drove. At that time, I was the mere age of twelve. All of a sudden Roy stopped the car and said, "Jock, you are going to drive." I was dumbfounded. I thought, with four in the floor, the clutch, the brake, how in the world could I do it?

Anyway, he moved me into the driver's seat, he got out and said to me, "OK, it is all yours." He did show me 1st, 2nd, and drive. He did not mention reverse. It was dark as pitch and we were in front of a large house with large oak trees in the front. I put my foot on the clutch, put it in gear and hit the foot feed a bit too hard and can you believe I had it in reverse.

Well, before I could get on the brake I backed into a large oak tree, bending Dad's left fender. Of course Roy was distraught with me and said, "Now look what you have done! Dad will surely whip us both."

You know, when we got home and told Dad, he was really nice and said, "Well boys, we will have to get it fixed."

My brother Roy, the eldest, decided he had had all the high school he needed, enlisted in the Army Air Corps and served about six months at an air base in Texas. Getting homesick, he decided he wanted out, and at that time you could get bought out with a sum of money. Well, Dad did just that. He borrowed the money. As I remember it must have been about $300, which was a lot of money.

About six months later Roy married a girl by the name of Juanita from Eldorado, Ar. Well, during this period dad died and things were tough.

CHAPTER 3

DAD AND INTEGRITY

I could not pass up the workings of the Great Depression that was all about housing. Only the very elite had the wealth and resources to build a house and, by today's standards, these homes were not near the quality or the footage that we see today.

For Dad, being a debit insurance salesman, his earnings were meager but he still had a vision of owning his own home.

We often hear the words, integrity and commitment. I did not learn the meaning of these words from books, I learned it from the adults whom I was privileged to be around in school and at home. For instance, in the middle of the Great Depression, my dad decided he was going to buy us a house. The price of the house was $600 with $50 down and so much each year until the balance was paid.

I remember well, as a youngster, going with my dad to the house of the man who owned the house my dad was buying. Upon knocking on the man's front door, dad and I waited and finally the man came to the door. My dad gave the man the $50 and they shook hands on the rest of the deal, with the understanding that if there ever came a time my dad could not make his payment, he would come to the man and ask out of the agreement.

In those days, if you wanted to go somewhere in a city of 1,200 persons, you would start walking, check out the surroundings and return home the same way. So we walked to the new house.

My brothers and I could not wait to see this house. Upon getting there we walked around the house and it was, what you would call today a "shotgun house." It consisted of four walls and a roof, with a front and back door with windows of single pane glass.

I can remember very well that the house was shaded on one side by huge pecan trees that had been planted years before. There was a large living room as you entered the front door and a large kitchen in the back with a hall leading to it. Off of the hall were three bedrooms, one for mom and dad and two more for us four boys.

Honestly, we thought that we had almost made heaven. We moved into the home and were there, as I recall, a total of about 5 years. We were so happy to have a roof over our heads and three meals a day, especially at the age of 10.

Well, about 4-5 years into the deal, Dad's Bright's disease, which he contracted during WWI, had made him very ill.

Dad decided, because of his illness, he could not make the purchase work, so we again went to the man's house, my dad told him that, due to the present circumstances, he could not continue the program.

This was prior to WWII, the depression was in full gear and we found the cheapest house we could rent and we moved. At night in this abode you could actually see the stars at times through the shingles.

There was no bathtub and the only way to get a bath was a wash tub. You can imagine that cold tub against your back as your mom poured hot water into the tub to make the cold water tolerable.

At this time, Dad became so ill that we transported him to the Army and Navy Hospital in Hot Springs, where he passed away about three weeks later.

This was in 1939 when my dad, Roy Cecil Davis, Sr. passed away. Bright's disease was a fatal kidney disease and I understand today it can be cured with a shot. He had spent quite some time in the old Army and Navy Hospital in Hot Springs because he was a veteran and had a service connected disability.

He and most of my family are buried at Prescott, AR, in the DeAnn cemetery.

CHAPTER 4

HARD TIMES AND A LOVING MOTHER

Things got bad after Dad passed away. There were 3 of us boys left at home. At this time meals were slim. I remember that Mom called Ed, my second oldest brother, into the kitchen and told him that she was going to sign up for relief. Well, this meant that you had to go to the court house, stand in line and receive your portion of dried milk, grapefruit juice, cheese and other items.

I felt sorry for her because she knew we would be embarrassed with our friends seeing us carry these items home. Well, we were embarrassed and mom never did ask us to pick up supplies again.

To give you some idea of what meals were like in that day, many times we would have hot cornbread with cow's butter and sorghum molasses. Seldom did we have eggs and very seldom did we have meat with the exception of Sunday and on that day it would be Mom's fried chicken from her chicken yard, mashed potatoes, gravy and biscuits. Now that was some "good eatin'". For dessert we would have vinegar cobbler or sweet potato pie. Both were very good.

*****

Just when you thought you could not handle any more, World War II happened with the Japanese attacking Pearl Harbor on December 7, 1941.

My old-maid aunt, who lived with us, immediately went to work at Lone Star Arsenal in Texarkana, making unbelievable money for that time. Things began to turn around and before you could think about it, we moved to a more livable home.

The years following, the three of us finished high school, entered the military and lightened the load on my mom and my aunt.

After receiving my honorable discharge from the army, with the rank Sgt., I began to reflect on the life I had lived as a young man, in the depression, in a home of tremendous love from my mom, aunts and uncles. Never or hardly ever having spending money created a lot of time to be around the house and converse with Mom.

It wasn't anything uncommon, after having

supper, that mom would say, "Jock, come on back to the bedroom, I need to clean out your ears." She would take a bobby pin, a ladies hair-pin, put the dull end into my ear and pull out hard wax. Man, I hated this, but you did not say "NO" to your mom at anytime.

Another experience that I hated was in the fall, before school started, Mom gave us all a "cleaning out." She would give us a round of purgative to clean us out and this would protect against sickness throughout the school year. Mom is in a better world today, but, if she were here I would tell her that her remedy did little good.

In relishing the love in our family and embracing each other any time we met, we always loved going home because that was the way we were greeted. How lovely it would be if we could see more of that today in the home.

CHAPTER 5

HIGH SCHOOL AND SPORTS

Those high school years are ones that I will never forget. As I remember, I had three jobs while in high school.

I was very fortunate to have a Kroger in my home town. The manager of the store was Mr. Raymond Hillis, a native of Atkins, Arkansas. I visited with him one day about working in the store before school, after school and on Saturdays. No stores were open on Sundays. I do not remember the pay per hour but compared to the money kids make today, it was nothing.

I will never forget one day, while I was working my shift at Kroger, a black lady came in and I asked her if I could help her. She said, "I would like three cans of EVA - P0 - RATED milk, two pounds of LORNA sausages, and two rolls of closet paper." Well, I was so taken back that I excused myself and asked Mr. Hillis what she wanted.

He replied, "Jock, she simply wants two rolls of toilet paper, two pounds of bologna and three cans of pet milk." I took care of the lady and learned a lot about my vocabulary that day. I also learned how to make sausage and cut meat.

Seldom did we have lettuce at home, so, when I had a break, I would take a head of lettuce, cut it in four wedges and eat one wedge per day. To this day I love lettuce.

Another job that I had was to ice box cars that were loaded with peaches and then delivered up north. This was normally in June and boy was it hot. There was a three story ice plant that stored ice all winter and was ready for the boxcars in the summer. Our shift ran from 10:00 P.M. until 6:00 A.M.

Ice, in 300 pound blocks would come down a chain out of the ice plant to the first available box car. The blocks came down at a pretty good speed and, when they arrived at your station, you would take a cant hook, which is a long pole with a sharp hook and point on the end of it, grab the 300 pound block, and shove it down a metal slide into the top hole that was situated at both ends of the boxcar.

Myself and the other high school boys enjoyed this work because it was cool work at that time of the morning and we had all the free peaches that we could eat.

One evening my buddies and I had the idea that we would jump into one of their A Model

Fords, go out to a watermelon field, lift a few watermelons, bring them back and put them in the ice house for cooling down. Little did we know that the owner was lying in wait in the field and as we jumped from the running boards and through a barbed wire fence to fetch the melons, the farmer jumped up and began firing a double-barrel shotgun into the air.

It did not take long to clear the barb wire fence, get on the running board and fly off down the road. This experience was a lasting experience and one I had just as soon forget. However, fate won out, someone had brought several melons to the ice house and we had a big feed for all of our guys.

The third of my jobs was at a stave mill which I mentioned in the previous chapter. We made wooden staves which were then made into whiskey barrels.

Everyone who lived in town walked to school. I walked about a mile, rain or shine to and from school each day. I would walk to work at Kroger, then to school, then to football practice, to work again and then walk the mile home after work.

I kept my grades up, even though the schedule was taxing. I even had time to mow yards on weekends to make school book and clothing money.

In those days we were fortunate to have one pair of shoes per year and they lasted such a short time because of the thread that was used to sew them. My mom would run baling wire through the sole and twist it. The sound the shoes made was distinctive and she would know me when I was walking home after dark kicking gravel.

*****

As we all grew and entered high school, the thing to do was play football. I loved sports. All four of us played high school sports, which, at that time was only football, basketball and track.

There was no encouragement from my mom. My mother never attended a game of any sort because she was trying to figure out what the next meal would be.

I lettered three years in basketball and football. One game in particular I will never forget was against Smackover. We had heard a lot about Clyde (Smackover) Scott from our coaches. He was a phenom in football and was to finally go to the University of Arkansas, play for Navy during the war, and afterward run the hurdles with Harrison Dillard during the Olympics.

That night all I heard was whistles. Our ending score was 60-0. Clyde and his brothers Tracey and Bennie played in the backfield and could score at will.

My mom had given me a dose of "Salts" that morning before we drove to Smackover. Sometime during the game, a 200-pound guard hit me so hard that I messed my britches. I came running to the sidelines and told coach what had happened. Well, he did not need for me to tell him because he had a nose. He said, "Davis, get to the dressing room, get another uniform and get back as soon as possible." I answered the call and played the rest of the game.

During the 40's there were very few seniors because they had gone to war, so, that was the reason he needed me so badly.

*****

Typing was my best subject and I learned to type on an old Underwood clatter machine. I even used my skills from high school to my time spent during two wars and was able to excel in both areas. I even won the State Championship in Typing in my first year in college. I typed 105 words per minute without making a mistake. I am still using that skill today on my computer. I love to type.

As I've said, my dad passed away in 1939 with Bright's disease. Roy and Ed had moved on to their military careers. It fell my lot, as eldest of the two boys left at home, to help provide for my little brother and my mother.

My brother was entering junior high and I was a sophomore in high school. Those were dark days, but thanks to a loving mom, she kept loving and encouraging us in life to make something of ourselves.

Upon graduation from college, my mom was present and she was so proud of me because I was the first of my family to attain a degree.

CHAPTER 6

AN EPIC STORY

I have tried my very best to portray the life of a Depression Era family. Living in those trying times and still having love for one another, and trying to make a living, must have been, at times, an intolerable time for our mom and dad. There is no doubt in my mind that we were the "Greatest Generation." I am sure there are those who would like to study a normal family who lived during these times and here I am at the age of eighty-six, being able to tell my family's story.

The picture on the front of the book was taken by a local photographer in Prescott, Arkansas immediately after World War II and the four of us were back home. Roy, the eldest, on the left and Ed, seated on the right, were married, but John and I had not taken that step at this point.

As you can see, the double-breasted suit was the dress of the day and the broad, colorful ties were worn by everyone.

Again, when I view this picture, I still feel the love my deceased brothers had for me and yes, I miss them very much, with their hugs and humor that I remember so well while growing up.

History will show, or has shown, that right before and during WWII the depression was in full swing.

Before my Dad's death, he had bought a battery radio. A family gathering was all four of us boys, my mom and Aunt Hop sitting down and listening to the fight of Joe Lewis and Max Schmeling. I am here to tell you that was a really big deal.

After school, one of the highlights of our afternoons was to listen to Jack Armstrong, the All American Boy and The Lone Ranger. Of course, there was Lum and Abner for the whole family. Today we are inundated with TV and computers.

Speaking of the computer, can you believe, with the Webcam attached, I can see my grandsons in Iraq and Afghanistan and converse with them over the phone at the same time.

PART 2

THE SERVICE YEARS

CHAPTER 7

CAMP ABBOTT

My brother, Ed, was in the Army, just out of the CCC and in the Medical Corps at the Army/Navy Hospital in Hot Springs, Arkansas. He had been assigned there for about a year before Pearl Harbor.

After about six months, being an avid model airplane builder and very interested in airplanes, Ed took the test to be a pilot. He passed the test with flying colors and began flight training in El Paso, Texas, flying an AT-6, which closely resembled a Stearman, a two cockpit bi-plane.

Ed, while stationed in Hot Springs, AR, met a registered nurse named Barbara, who was in training at the St. Joseph Hospital. After they married, Barbara stayed on in her job while Ed stayed in training in El Paso.

I can tell you one thing, from the pictures I saw of Ed during flight training, he was put through the grind. He had lost so much weight but was right there at the top of his class in flight training. Finally, he received his wings and had sights on multi-engine bombers and was assigned to the initial B-26.

This bomber, in its infancy, was so prone to crash, in fact, it was named, "the flying coffin." Once they corrected some of the faults it became a real threat in skip-bombing.

Ed was sent to London, and flew out of there most of the time while overseas. He did a lot of skip-bombing over the dikes in Holland.

About this time my brother, Roy, had married and gone through a divorce and had joined the Marines right after Pearl Harbor. He was a drill instructor at Texas A & M and rose quickly to Sgt., which, at that time was quite an achievement, considering that he was a non-combatant Marine.

At that time, Dad had been dead about two years and I was a junior in high school and my baby brother was four years behind me. At least there were only two boys to feed instead of four. My two older brothers helped as much as they could, but on a private's pay there was little to send home. Mom did have a small pension that dad left, from a service connected injury he received in a battle in the Argonne Forest in France in WWI.

And then my time came. Finally, I registered while underage in September 1943, and was called to active duty in October of 1943.

After a final type physical, I was bussed to Camp Robinson in Little Rock. My hair was cut off, I was given oversized boots and clothing, was told that I would grow into them, was taught to salute, and I was ready to serve my country.

Boy, was I excited. I couldn't wait to earn ribbons and medals. At the mere age of eighteen, I left my mom, my little brother and was off to the war.

We were all loaded on a troop train right there in Camp Robinson and started a long trip to basic training at a camp. We knew not where we were going. We just did what we were told.

After about three days of travel, our train load of soldiers arrived in Bend, Oregon. After disembarking, we were placed on busses and bussed to Camp Abbot. This camp was a combat engineer camp where we were to spend the next six weeks readying for combat either in the Pacific or European theatre.

Camp Abbott was a beautiful camp with large trees. The Deschutes River was nearby and there was plenty of snow. (Today I understand that Camp Abbott is a retirement area for the elderly.)

A typical day consisted of getting up at 5:00 A.M., falling in for roll call in the snow, then breakfast before greeting a day of physical training, the rifle range, and hikes. All of this with no weekends off.

The clothing was warm but not overly so, but being young has its attributes and being physically fit was helpful for all the physical training that was required. It was like, "Bring it on boys."

*****

Little did we know that the insignia of the engineers was a castle. Upon entering the confines of the camp, we had to pass under a hand-hewn log castle, just like the one that would appear on our dress Olive Drab Uniform.

My days and nights at Camp Abbott were short. I will never forget my first lesson in making my bed, instructed by my drill corporal. We all gathered in the barracks that first day to witness perfection at its best with bed making. The Corporal shouted, "Listen up draftees. I will give you one instruction and one instruction only. When I have finished making this bed, each of you will go to your bed, place the sheets and blankets on properly with the hospital fold, flip a fifty cent piece and if it doesn't bounce up properly, you will have extra duty."

Well, he went through the routine and in my sight it was simple because I had learned to make a hospital fold on the corners when I was home.

We all started at the same time and when finished the Corporal came by flipping the coin and when all was said and done, only two out of the barracks failed the test and had extra duty.

When I was younger, one thing mom demanded was that our beds be made up and we would either throw our dirty clothing in a laundry basket or hang it up. Therefore lining up my clothing in my assigned area and taking care of my foot locker was not a problem.

*****

It was October and already snowing at camp. We began a vigorous campaign of strenuous PT and those of us right out of high school, especially those of us who played sports, thought it was fun to run the course, climb the wall, and swing on the rope across the pond.

The PT program was very taxing. Many of our counterparts of greater age had a difficult time running the course.

Next was the rifle range, using the M-1 Garand, a 30-caliber rifle with clip. The first thing we had to do was clean the cosmoline off of the weapon, then oil it well before we fired it. During the course of training I fired a sharpshooter score with the temperature at five below zero and a blowing snow storm. I was thrilled with my score.

The food was great but we all missed home, even though we were kept busy. I found out soon enough that you do not "short cut food" at the family style dining. One day, the pinto beans were being passed to the Sergeant just beyond me and I stopped the bowl and started to help myself when all of a sudden the bowl of beans was in my lap. I never did make that mistake again.

I suppose my favorite meal was breakfast. The eggs, as you like them, with sausage and bacon, was my favorite. Of course my real desire was for their S--- on the shingle. That stands for gravy made with beef or sausage poured over toast. No one could make it like the army.

*****

Two things I vividly remember about basic training. One was of how homesick I was at Christmas time and the second was the 20-mile forced hike in parkas.

Being only 18 years of age and coming from a very poor but a very loving home made Christmas much more important because we all knew we were going overseas after basic. I cried myself to sleep every night listening to Bing Crosby sing "White Christmas" over the loud speakers around the camp.

I attended church in the camp chapel and even visited the Chaplain for consolation, which did not help a bit.

*****

The second thing was the 20-mile forced march which started out early one morning. We climbed to the top of a mountain, which was ten miles, and dug prone shelters in the snow and frozen tundra with our entrenching tools. That night we lay in our sleeping bags in the holes and covered ourselves with shelter halves to prevent the snow from covering us. Well, surprisingly, I slept well and when I awoke the next morning for the ten-mile trek back to camp,

I found that I was under about four inches of snow. It was a trying time but no one complained and we moved on to the next adventure.

*****

I recall that there was one young man about twenty years old who had the worst body odor I had ever witnessed. He was a big guy. Five of us grabbed him one weekend night, tied him up, carried him to the company shower up the street and scrubbed him with a rough floor brush using that old lye soap as a cleanser. The poor guy was as red as a tomato when we finished with him but he was clean. The rest of the time we were there, he was always the first in the shower.

*****

Then there was the time that the Corporal picked me to be the barracks orderly for the day. I was informed that I would mop the wooden floor, clean the windows and have a warm fire going in the coal stove that heated the barracks. Well, our squad wasn't out of sight when I began to mop and clean. When I was through with cleaning the floor and windows it was about noon. The troops would be in about five in the afternoon from hiking in the snow and would be very cold.

My next task was to build a coal fire. I had never seen a coal stove, much less built a fire in one. I had never been instructed and knew nothing about it. I thought by stuffing newspapers in the stove and pouring coal in on top that it would start.

Well, I was worried to death: it was four in the afternoon, the barracks was cold and there was no fire in the coal stove. At five, the troops poured into the barracks and began shouting, "This building is cold."

Here came the corporal and he yelled, "Davis, what in the he-- have you been doing all day?" I said, "Trying to build a coal fire, sir." I was given an instructor who hailed from coal country and he was given the task of teaching me how to build a coal fire. Well, the secret was kindling. The fire was started and the building warmed.

The next day I was given the duty of cleaning the shower every night for a week, which meant I couldn't even go to town. These are examples of what goes on in the life of a young man, eighteen years of age and a buck private in the army.

I can tell you that you grow to be a man immediately. You are responsible for yourself and no one is there to comfort you, or feel sorry for you.

One thing that I found that I had and that was the freedom to read my Bible and to pray before I closed my eyes at night.

*****

I honestly believe that the most moving thing of my training was our graduation parade. Two weeks before graduation, the Corporal asked me to carry the Guidon which was a flag on a staff that indicated our unit and I would walk at the front right of our column setting the speed of march and everyone had to keep step with me. I was so proud to walk behind Old Glory, with the band blaring, "Stars and Stripes Forever."

I knew that wherever I was headed, I was physically ready for the job. I knew how to shoot my M-1 Garand 30-caliber rifle, I knew every working part of it. I knew how to pack my backpack properly, I knew every working part of close order drill, and I knew what it meant to NOT short-cut the food in the dining hall. I knew how to make a coal fire in the barracks, I could read a map and I knew what a perimeter was. I could set off explosives under a bridge or under water. I knew the workings of a Bailey Bridge and its purpose. I knew the engineer's song, "A Rambling Wreck from Georgia Tech." I knew first-aid as it applied to wounds in time of war and knew exactly where my first-aid kit was at all times. I had the perfect salute down to a perfect art and would never be caught again with my hands in my pockets. I knew a perfectly made bunk when I saw one and I cared for all my buddies as if they were my brothers.

I learned that self-discipline, commitment and integrity were the main ingredients in making a successful life. I also learned that things do not just happen, they are brought about. Believing in a higher Supreme Being makes life for everyone more beautiful. I could not have endured those months of training, cold and hardships without God.

I knew that there was a mission awaiting me but I did not know what it was. I knew that after my furlough home, of two weeks duration, I would be put on a train and shipped overseas. I just prayed that each day I would be taken care of and that I would do my very best for my country, my family and that my buddies would be proud of me.

Little did I know what awaited me the next two and a half years. It would have made little difference however.

Finally the time came for our two-week furlough home. Each of us said farewell to our buddies and caught the nearest train home.

*****

I rode a bus to Boise, Idaho, caught a train and it took me three days to get home. On the bus ride to Boise, which took about four hours, I met a beautiful young lady, about my age. We visited about where I was from and where I was probably going. We talked about how rough it was to be away from home and the uncertainty of the future.

We talked about many things that related to life and before I left the bus I asked her if I could kiss her. She replied, "You certainly may." I obliged her with the best kiss I was capable of giving. Upon reaching Boise, this young lady bade me farewell. I stepped off the bus and onto the train and never saw or heard of this young lady again. I know that she felt deeply about the war effort and that I might not be coming back. She felt it would be the thing for her to do, to give me that kiss.

One thing that stands out in my memory about the long train ride home was a layover in Denver, Colorado. I had a twenty dollar bill and needed a coke. I gave the lady the twenty, she gave me back nineteen silver dollars and some change. I can tell you one thing, nineteen silver dollars weigh a lot. These were not Eisenhower dollars, they were silver Walking Liberties. I do wish I had those silver dollars today for a keepsake.

The ride on home was uneventful and I stepped off on the platform at Prescott, Arkansas, walked with my duffel bag to my home and was greeted.

At this time, my two older brothers were engaged in military careers of their own. Ed, my second eldest brother was overseas flying a B-26 bomber over Holland and my eldest brother, Roy, was stationed at Texas A&M university as a Drill Sgt. in the Marines.

My baby brother, John Edsel - we called him "Sook" - was a sophomore in high school in

Prescott, helping Mom get by and finishing high school.

2nd Lt. Edward Davis preparing to make another practice flight in his primary trainer in 1942

CHAPTER 8

NEW GUINEA

After my furlough, I was transported by train again to Camp Stoneman in California for shipment overseas.

After one week of preparation for the South Pacific, we were transported to the docks and set sail for places unknown. The ship I was on held 600 Army personnel, plus a full Navy crew. The trip took thirty days to travel from California to Oro Bay, New Guinea.

I believe jungle fever and reptiles were much more feared than the Japanese. The Ubangi natives were small in size, had no teeth (due to chewing beetle nuts) and wore nothing from the waist up. It was not an uncommon sight to see a mother walking down the road with a small child sitting on her hip, nursing.

Atabrine was given to all of us each day to ward off Malaria.

*****

During WWII it took a package or letter about 30 days to get to New Guinea and the same amount of time for a letter to get to my family back home.

I remember well one Christmas when I received a box from my mom. It was ninety degrees and muggy when my package came. It had been shipped in November and arrived around Christmas time. All of my buddies sat on the edge of their cots as I slowly unwrapped the gift of Christmas from my mom.

There, in a large pan with the top closed and tightly sealed with some sort of tape, was something that I had yearned for. It was my favorite cake, fruitcake, and when I removed the sealed top the aroma nearly took my head off. Mom always cooked with rum and it was loaded. Well, this was my dream, this beautiful, black Christmas fruit cake that no one but my mom could bake.

My buddies kept chiding me, "Hurry up." And when I removed the lid, that smell of rum roared through their nostrils as well as mine. Of course, my buddies, all five of them, just had to have a piece. The taste was tantalizing and to preserve the longevity of the cake, small portions were meted out to each guy.

We met each day at lunch at the same time and ate as long as the cake lasted. Oh, how delicious and how wonderful that cake was and I could not wait to get a V-Mail off to my mom explaining how my buddies and I loved every morsel. I want to tell you that, even though it took about forty days to get to me, my buddies and I made ourselves sick over that cake.

*****

Well, every day was the same and it wasn't just five days a week. We worked as though Sunday was a work day but the Chaplain always had a service for everyone. I am sure there were men there who had never entered the doors of a church, but because they could be off from work detail for an hour or two, they came and several were saved.

About all the entertainment we had was to hear a buddy read a letter from home or we sat under a coconut tree and watched a P-38 fighter knock a Jap Zero out of the sky and into the bay. As time went on there were fewer dog fights due to the ineptness of the Zero fighters.

After about six months of this jungle torture, I awoke one night with a very high fever. I had never felt this way before. The next morning, with my head bursting, I asked the Sergeant to get me to a doctor. He knew there was something bad wrong with me. He put me in a jeep and drove for what seemed like hours to a field hospital.

My blood pressure and temperature was taken. I could tell that the nurse was surprised by the look in her eyes when she saw the thermometer. She put me in a gown and got me into a hospital bed and gave me something by mouth and began placing cool water patches on my forehead. From that time forward I knew nothing for about four days.

About the sixth day, a Doctor, who was a Captain, came by and told me that I had contracted a jungle fever, called Dengue fever, and sometimes it was fatal but I had made it and that I would be leaving the islands for Melbourne, Australia. I have never heard such sweet words in my life.

I was picked up the next day with all of my belongings and transported to the shore with others like me and we rode out to a beautiful ship. An elevator-type device was lowered to the DUKW. We were plucked out of the DUKW and were placed on board this ship. I did not know it then but this was a luxury liner. We were given a state room, two men to a room with deck portholes to enjoy the cool ocean air and see the sights. I honestly thought that I was dreaming.

We had waiters waiting on us in dress tuxes, if you can believe it. Keep in mind that this was a time of war and submarines were lurking everywhere because we were not too far from Japan at that point.

Our sea journey took about seven days. We docked offshore at Melbourne and there were trucks there to deliver us to our new assignments.

CHAPTER 9

AUSTRALIA

My wish is that everyone in America could have an opportunity to spend a year in Australia, especially Melbourne. There are so many memories that persist from my war years. The Koala bears, the Botanical Gardens, swimming on St. Kilda beach at America's Christmas time, shopping downtown Melbourne, watching the Kangaroos perform at the local museum. The sights just overwhelm you.

The young ladies of Australia were very beautiful. I was dating a young lady and after attending a concert one evening and returning to her house, she complained about her "plates" hurting her gums. I was taken aback at this remark but after further questioning I found that practically all of the young people lost their teeth early due to the lack of fluoride.

I mentioned to my wife that I wish we could visit Australia sometime. She responded that the young ladies I knew in 1944 did not look the same as they did then.

*****

After reaching Australia, I was assigned to an Engineer Topographic Battalion. This unit was making and shipping maps of all sizes, types and colors to regions to be used in battle. We were even printing silk maps for the pilots to use in flight. The unit was designed to manufacture maps for the next landing, eventually leading up to an invasion of Japan, which never happened because of the bomb.

A three-story warehouse had been turned into a topographic haven. There were floors for draftsmen and for living quarters. There were floors for dining facilities and land floors for the presses. We always had a security guard at the front door.

We were housed in this three-story warehouse with billeting,showers, and a mess hall. It was very nice. It was a welcome change from where I had just served.

At that time, I was still eighteen years of age and was the youngest soldier out of three hundred fifty men. I was assigned the name of "Little Dave" and most of the guys serving were surveyors and engineers in civilian life. Most of them were heavy in age, I mean the oldest being 38 and from there down.

We always knew when the next invasion

would be according to the maps that were being flown to that particular area by a C-47 aircraft, which was the workhorse for the Army Air Corps. By the way, I did have the opportunity of flying in one of these aircraft.

I was a Corporal and was the Company Clerk. My job was to make the morning report, which consisted of quite a bit of paperwork that had to be done the very first thing.

The First Sergeant was named Sergeant Puncsak, a polish ex-boxer who expected the best out of everyone. If one of the enlisted men wanted to question a decision of his, he would take them out in the alley, they would take off their stripes, (or their shirts) and go to fist city and the matter was settled. There was always a black eye here and there. Sergeant Puncsak was always good to me in everything I did as his company clerk.

I was fortunate to be able to help transport the maps to the airport, load them on a C-47 and see the plane take off for the islands, knowing where the next landing would be.

Each afternoon, we would walk back from the airport, which was about a half mile to our building and along the way my buddies would have to stop by a pub for a beer.

Melbourne was the first place that I had tasted alcohol and it was a miserable memory. Roy Pomrenke, Private First Class and the oldest member of the unit at age 38, from Peoria, Illinois, told me on Saturday morning that he had us a date with two cuties for a dance that night and had bought two bottles of wine. I said, "OK." And we were off.

We caught a cab, picked up the girls and went to the dance. At that time I prided myself in being a very good Jitterbug dancer and Australia had records of bands like Glenn Miller and Artie Shaw. I danced and I drank, and I danced and I drank.

Well, about two hours later I told Roy that I did not feel good and that we needed to start back to our building. He said "OK", we took the girls home and went straight back to our building in the cab.

As quickly as I could, I took off my uniform, and laid down on the top bunk where I slept. Sometime within the hour I awoke with the bunk swirling, or at least I thought it was. Somehow, I fell out of my bunk to the floor and made my way to the latrine. I must tell you that everything from years past came up, over and over. Well, I was so weak I could hardly make it back to my bunk but I did.

Upon rising in the morning ready for work, I was so thirsty I could hardly stand it. I went to the nearest fountain and loaded up on water. Again, I felt as I did the night before. I was again "Lit Up" and this carried on for two days. I will testify to the fact that from that very hour until this day I have never again tasted wine and never will.

*****

I can say that the Australian people were very fond of the American soldier. The news of General MacArthur leaving the Philippines and being thoroughly involved with the Australian Government was something everyone knew and they had all the respect in the world for General MacArthur.

*****

One of the highlights of my Australia visit during the war was being invited by one of the Aussie families to spend the weekend with them.

A family by the name of Edwards invited a young man named Ybarra, who was of Spanish descent, and I to their home.

I will never forget thinking while Ybarra and I rode on the electric train out to the Edwards home that probably the first thing we would be served would be mutton. I will explain later what I meant by this statement.

Well, after being greeted with a hearty greeting by two of the Edwards children at the train station, we rode to their home. We were shown our bedroom and we prepared to have dinner with them.

What do you know! I looked at Ybarra and he looked at me, for there was a large platter of lamb chops right in the middle of the table. I could not believe the delicate taste of the chops and everything that went with them. I did praise Mrs. Edwards for the fine meal and explained why we were worried about them having Mutton.

I told the story about our Army cooks not being able to cook mutton properly. When you walked into the mess hall and mutton was cooking, you immediately said, "NO WAY." It was so bad that the cooks would have so much mutton left over that they would try to serve it as stew. I can tell you today that I have never eaten mutton since my war days.

*****

We were paid in Australian pounds and, at that time, American money was worth much more. On payday, even though my pay was around thirty-five dollars, in Aussie Pounds that was a lot of money.

The Australian "digger" or soldier was jealous of the American soldier. Their pay was much less than ours, therefore, the American G.I. could afford nice things for the Aussie ladies. In fact, an American G.I. could take his pick of the beautiful Australian ladies. This made for a very uncomfortable feeling when an American G.I. and his girlfriend would meet a digger and his girlfriend walking down the street.

I remember that over a third of our soldiers were married to Aussie girls. The ones who were married spent evenings at their spouse's home.

In several cases, I knew of unwanted pregnancies that happened out of wedlock. I remember one day a young lady and her mother came to the front door and asked the security guard to speak with one of the soldiers. The guard left, went upstairs and returned in a few minutes and gave the two ladies the sad story.

The soldier whom they had asked for had been shipped back to the United States. I will never know if the soldier did indeed go back to the U.S. or this was a deal that was made between the guard and the soldier. I am sure there were other cases such as this that existed, but I knew nothing of it.

CHAPTER 10

PHILIPPINES

Well, all good things must come to an end, so one day the Battalion Commander called the entire Battalion together and informed us that we were moving so fast toward Japan that we would be moving up within thirty days.

We were given our assignments on packing our materials and personal belongings and loaded on trucks bound for the docks.

There again awaited us a troop ship of the same design I came over on to New Guinea. We were assigned a bunk, given the same regulations basically that we received when we left San Francisco. We had no idea where we were going, how long it would take, nor the conditions we would be faced with.

But my stint in the Philippines was so different. Upon our troop ship docking in Manila Harbor, we were all looking overboard and saw about fifty little boys swimming around the ship asking the G.I.'s to throw coins overboard and they would try to grab them before they sank to the bottom of the harbor. Not many of the coins sank. I could not believe how these young boys could grab those coins so fast to keep them from sinking.

The Japanese had been driven about two miles from downtown Manila and we had been informed we would be housed right in the middle of the city in another three-story building carrying the name of Aguanaldo. This building was one of only a few that was still standing when the Americans finished their bombing runs. This building was the place that our TOPO outfit would do their drafting and printing of the maps that would eventually find their way to Okinawa and even deeper toward the cities of Japan.

About three hundred yards from this building was a large manufacturing building that was being outfitted for our billeting. We were all shown the building and assigned bunks in triple-deckers and then shown where we would shower, shave, and eat. Little did I know that this would be my home for over a year and a half.

I remember seeing the ladies who lived in makeshift hutches beating their clothes with rocks alongside a river that ran through downtown Manila. I can still see young boys and girls pilfering garbage piles for something to eat and placing what they found in a small bucket to take back home for their family. Before the war, Manila was a beautiful city but after the bombings there was nothing but bricks and rubble.

Of course, we worked seven days per week, and so did our fellow combatants. We did take time out to observe Christian services, conducted by the chaplains. We had a makeshift PX and we were able to buy toiletries and other items that we needed. We walked to and from work.

I can still remember our barracks adopting a stray monkey. His name was Jocko, not named after me; my name was "Jock" and is to this day. "Jocko" was tied to a rope that was tied to a cable which ran the length of the barracks, which was about 200 feet long. Upon our arrival back from work in the afternoons, "Jocko" would scream and fly from one end of the barracks to the other.

The sad story of this was that one afternoon, as we approached the barracks, there was no screaming. "Jocko" had accidentally missed the cable in a long leap and hanged himself. Of course there was a service held for "Jocko" and he was never replaced.

My buddies and I would often travel to the front lines outside of Manila to observe the battle. As we would approach, on foot, we would walk over many dead Japanese soldiers, who had lain on the battlefield so long that the oils from their skin was showing through their uniforms from the hot sun that was burning down from the sky. I couldn't help but think about this young man, even a Jap, who was dead and his mother had not yet been notified.

During my stay here, we were cautioned about drinking Saki that was left behind by the "Japs." It could have been injected with a hypodermic needle flowing with poison. I knew of one man in our unit that did not heed the advice and died from poisoning.

During our most recent wars in Iraq and Afghanistan, we hear of our boys being counseled when they get home from battle fatigue. One evening, one of our own men portrayed himself as a motor boat by getting in a long sink with his shorts on and sliding the entire length of the sink making sounds like that of a motor boat. He was sent home for treatment and I never heard from him again.

We worked hard, the days and nights passed slow and of course the idea of getting a V-Mail from home was exciting. Remember, it took 30 days, or thereabout, to receive a package or letter.

Prayer and Bible reading was the order of the day for most of the troops. Of course, this was not required but we who were Christians knew this was the thing to do if we wanted to see the States again.

Finally, the bomb was dropped. Word came to us immediately and there was rejoicing in the streets of Manila. Right across the street from our work place was General MacArthur's Headquarters. I have seen the General exit his headquarters, enter his top-down military vehicle with three MP's aboard and careen off down the streets of Manila.

There are other stories of the Walled City where the General served until the Japanese invaded Manila and blew the Walled City away, destroying the General's gold plated dinnerware and other valuables. I can tell you that, after surveying the Walled City after the Americans reoccupied Manila, what was left of the Walled City was a pile of bricks.

I have visited Corregidor and witnessed the area of the death march of many gallant Army Soldiers of the United States. It was heartbreaking to walk where they walked. I do not carry animosity today toward the Japanese, but their methods of extracting information from our troops was inhumane and our memories of these methods remain with the World War II Veterans today.

*****

What wonderful three words I heard when my Sergeant said one day, "You're going home." I had gained the points I needed to board a ship and head for the good old USA.

Those of us who had enough points to go home were housed in tents. We were asked, while waiting for our ship to pull in, to stand in front of our tents each morning on the Company Street in the nude, endure a short arm inspection, get our clothing back on and rest comfortably on our cots.

This took about a week and then we were boarded on a troop ship and started our four week trip back home. I can't begin to explain the happiness of these 600 men aboard this ship when hearing all of those ship horns when we pulled into port. We went topside and there was the glorious Golden Gate Bridge that we had passed under two years before, not knowing our destination or whether we would see this sight again.

We were taken to Camp Stoneman in California, given a royal dinner and spent the next six days preparing for our long journey home on a troop train.

The troop train pulled up right into the middle of Camp Stoneman. We boarded the train and headed for Arkansas. Three days later this train entered Fort Chaffee in Arkansas. We were dismissed from the train and placed in barracks where we would undergo a week of debriefings to get us ready to enter civilian life once again.

During these debriefings, things were promised such as future health care, payment by check for about the first year and many other promises that never materialized.

Finally, I was given my ticket to the train heading to my home town, given a final Army meal, and then I was off to Prescott, Arkansas.

I arrived home about eleven o'clock that night, with just my uniform, a duffel bag with a few military clothes, shaving kit and boots. I walked home, about twenty blocks. When I knocked, Mom came to the door and asked who was there and I said, "Your son, Jock." There was weeping and hugging such as I have never witnessed. I was finally home for good.

There were no bands playing, no one there to meet us, no one to say, "Well done, good and faithful servant." Just a feeling inside of me that said, "Well, I have done my very best for my country and thank you Lord for bringing me home safely."

Jock as a freshman at Arkansas Tech University

CHAPTER 11

ARKANSAS TECH UNIVERSITY

When I arrived home on the train from Ft. Chaffee, little did I know what would be in store for me the next four years.

Things at home were not the same. All of my friends were still in the Armed Services, killed during WWII or were already working some other place. There was nothing to do at home but sit and think about my past during the War.

About the first part of February, 1946, I received a call from one of my old buddies with whom I grew up, Alvin Reese. He asked what I was going to do now that I was home. Before answering him, I asked where he was and what he was doing. He responded that Bill Stainton and he, two of my high school buddies, were attending Arkansas Tech University in Russellville, Arkansas.

At that time, ATU was a Junior College and had an enrollment of about 600 students. It also had a great prep school in Forestry. Both Alvin and Bill were working on their Associate Degrees in Forestry and in two years would receive their degree and transfer to Monticello A&M, located in Monticello, Arkansas.

Alvin asked me to jump on a bus and take the ride through Hot Springs to Russellville and become enrolled at Tech. Well, with twenty four hours to study the situation, I told my mom of my desire and she was all for it. After all, the government paid for everything through the G.I. Bill, including spending money. Since I had no job and no prospects for one, this seemed the ideal thing to do.

I spent the next day telling everyone goodbye and packing up to move to Russellville, Arkansas. Packing up meant a rather large pasteboard box with cotton string tied around it. If my memory serves me right, Mom packed a hand sown quilt, two single sheets, a pillow case, my shaving kit, a new bar of soap, my combat boots and a pair of G.I. issue, low-quarter shoes.

The only clothing I had was my G.I. issue underwear, G.I. socks, an Army cloth belt, and the clothing I had on, which included an "Ike Jacket" for warmth. At that time, retail stores had very few garments for sale because clothing, like everything else, had "gone to war."

I kissed my mom goodbye and walked to the bus station with my box. I checked in, bought my ticket and waited for the bus that would take me into a life that turned out to be exceptionally rewarding.

*****

As I remember, I arrived at the bus station about two o'clock in the afternoon. After receiving a detailed description of how to get to Tech I was on my way.

From the bus station, I think the University was about a mile. I walked that mile with my pasteboard box on my shoulder and no one offered me a ride.

Upon arriving at Tech, I asked the direction to the Main Dorm, which at that time was the only dorm. With directions in hand, I set out to find Bill and Alvin.

Upon arriving at their dorm door, I knocked. Alvin opened the door and we had one very good hug. He asked me to come in and they would get me a cot to sleep on until I could get a room assigned the next day.

I must tell you that many questions went through my mind. I wondered if this was the right thing to do. I even wondered if I should go back to the bus station and head for home and seek a job at the Bemis Lumber Mill, which was where most of the vets sought jobs and received them. I finally fell asleep and let the questions go by.

The next morning, the three of us were up early and walked to the cafeteria for breakfast. After I was vouched for by my friend, Alvin, Mr. Fiser, the cafeteria manager, said it would be alright for me to eat breakfast.

My next move, after eight o'clock that morning, was to go to the registration office and register as a freshman for college. Mr. Turrentine was the Registrar and was a very nice, elderly man. I found that it was suggested that I enroll in the College of Business.

My load was sixteen hours and with being a Veteran, I was given two hours credit without taking P.E. This load was eighteen hours, with most of the courses being electives.

Upon being registered and given a room in main dorm, I was asked to visit the Veteran's Assistance Office for further information.

Dr. Hamm was the V.A. Assistance person and he was a prince of a fellow. He informed me that as long as I made passing grades and acted like a person of integrity, I could graduate in two years. Little did I know that, back then, the government kept tabs on you.

The next move was to travel to the Techionary, to get all of my books and supplies, and I could start to school the next day, which was Tuesday. Please keep in mind that I was a month late in registering, but the college was not going to pass on a veteran, because there was a certain amount of funds that went to the university from the government. They just were not going to miss out on a student.

The Techionary was both a book store and a place for the students to gather in booths to jitterbug and visit between classes. I knew at that point that this was the place for me because I loved to jitterbug.

The thing about college in those days was, it wasn't uncommon to see a lot of vets with their woolen, Olive Drab pants and shirts walking to class or just on campus. Remember, civilian clothing had gone to war and had not returned.

The first guy that I met on campus, other than my buddies, was Don Dover. Don was a WWII Veteran and a freshman. We spent a lot of time together, double-dating, having a few and just hanging out. Don is still alive and lives in Conway, Arkansas. His wife "Curly" passed away about three years ago and we still visit over the phone and in person.

In 1946 there was a beer parlor in downtown Russellville and it was a place for folks, especially Veterans, to hang out at the end of day. Speaking of the beer parlor, there was a Chemistry Professor by the name of Dr. Bock on staff at the college. At the end of day, Dr. Bock would travel to the beer parlor, sit at one of the tables, drink beer and grade Chemistry papers. I do not know if it is true or not but it was said that Dr. Bock's chemistry students, mostly boys, helped him grade the test papers at the parlor.

*****

It took almost a year for me to be able to get clothes in my closet. I did find myself a pair of brown and white Saddle Oxfords that I wore to all the dances.

My first year passed and my grades were not anything to write home about. There was one thing that I was proud of, though. My typing instructor had noticed that my finger dexterity was very good when it came to typing. She came to me one day and said, "Mr. Davis, would you enter a competition on speed typing on the state level? I told her I would if she would help me put all the pieces together and practice so that I could compete.

I traveled to Little Rock and entered the contest. When it was all over, I was crowned the state champion in speed typing with 105 words per minute and no mistakes. I still love to type today like I did then, except now I use a computer.

Again, I must share with you that it is very tough to leave a battlefield, instead of a high school, and go to college. It took me over a year to get to the point of settling down and knowing that if I was going to succeed in life, I must discipline myself and make good grades.

I must admit that I was summoned to the Veteran's office a few times that first year about every facet of my educational life at Arkansas Tech University.

When you have gone to war for three years and you test your discipline by sitting by a window on a beautiful spring day, you tend to think of all the things you have gone through in the past three years.

I know now that the best thing that ever happened to me was in the beginning of my second year when I met this beautiful little blond and started dating her.

From the first day that I saw her, checking in as a freshman at Arkansas Tech University, I knew this was the lady for me.

Even though I was a seasoned Army veteran of war and had the experience of serving overseas, I knew Melba Jean Thompson was the one. I know it was not a fairy tale meeting but the romance that started out with "maybe" continues after sixty-two years of happiness.

It seemed an eternity before she ever agreed to date me. After we started dating, I asked her to go to a football game with me one evening. Well, on the evening of the game, which was a very cold evening in November, I went to her dorm and we walked to the stadium, which was about three hundred yards away.

Earlier that afternoon, before the game, I had asked one of my buddies to drive me to Dardanelle, a wet county, and I picked up a pint of Jack Daniels. Someone had either given me an overcoat, or I had borrowed one, and I had placed this pint in the inside pocket of the overcoat. Before I picked Melba up, I placed a straw in the top of the bottle where I could take a sip now and then when the game was going. Everything went well until the game was over and I tried to help her down from way up in the stands. Well, in retrospect, she helped me down, because she thought I was "ill".

After that date I was fortunate that she ever dated me again. In fact it was several weeks before she would consent to another date and I made sure that she knew that that incident would never happen again, and it did not.

Little did I know at the time that this person would direct my steps positively, leading me to be a success in life and in business.

Jock's beautiful wife, Melba

CHAPTER 12

MARRIED LIFE

Of course, with WWII behind me, and a college degree available for me, a devoted wife was my first step to success. You know the old saying "Behind every successful man, there is a woman, PUSHING." I know this is right in my case.

After dating for over a year on the campus, I asked Melba Jean Thompson to marry me and to my surprise, she said "Yes." We were married in a church in Morrilton, Arkansas, with two attendants. A friend of mine, who owned a cattle truck, then transported my new bride and I to Petit Jean Mountain, where we would spend a three-day honeymoon that would cost us the full sum of THIRTY-FIVE dollars.

Upon arrival back to campus, Melba and I rented a small fiber board trailer for newlyweds, most of them from the War, and this started my success story.

You have heard the words, "Getting accustomed to married life." You can really get accustomed to married life by living together in a small trailer that is eight feet wide and 20 feet long.

Looking back on those three years, it was good for both of us, having to budget our money, charging groceries at a little store on North Arkansas Avenue and even looking into the bottom of the old couch that was furnished, to find a dime to buy a loaf of bread. Yes, and we walked everywhere we wanted to go. At that time there were only two vehicles on the campus.

At the start of the new semester, Melba decided she would get a job in downtown Russellville. She applied for and got an administrative job at Plunkett-Jarrell Wholesale Grocery and worked there until I graduated from college.

Oh yes, there were plenty of opportunities if you wanted to work. Mr. Fiser was manager of the dining hall. I asked him for a job in my spare time and I was hired as a dishwasher. I enjoyed the monthworking with Cassie, an older black lady who everyone loved very much.

I also asked for and received a job from Col. Buerkle, for whom the ATU football field was named. I did odd jobs on the campus that related to maintenance. Col. Buerkle was head of the Engineering Department at Tech and it was a pleasure working for him those three years.

On top of this, I ran for Mayor of our trailer city and won. I received our trailer rent free and was in charge of all washing powder for the local coin laundry.

There were many happy hours visiting with other couples who lived in the trailer city. I will never forget, after living in the trailer city for about a year, a young couple fell in love, were married and moved next door to us. Their names were Jack and Dot Simpson. This couple was "getting accustomed to married life" in the small trailer and were arguing all the time, and in the springtime when the windows were open, you could hear every word.

One morning they were arguing and I told Melba that I was going next door and put a stop to it. I went through our door and was standing in front of Jack and Dot's screen door and opened my mouth to speak at the same time Jack ducked and I met a cup of hot coffee on my neck and chest. I must tell you that it was hot but that stopped the arguing with laughter from both of us.

Many funny things of this nature went on in the trailer city. We had many wonderful friends and we still talk of how tough those days were to get by on the money that the G.I. Bill paid.

There was a lot more to my college years than attending classes. Time spent in the trailer city was much more memorable than the time spent in those one-armed seats in the class room.

There was a creek that backed up to the campus. I have seen occasions when the trailer city on the back side of the campus had water in some of the trailers. At the close of a storm and torrential rains, it would even back up to our trailers.

The trailer city was well lit and one winter or early spring there was a huge flock of white geese that flew exceptionally low over the area that was flooded and our trailers.

Several of us stepped outside with our shotguns and cut loose. Several of the white geese fell right in the trailer city and we thought we had struck it rich. Well, we picked the birds, cooked them, and man were they tough, but it was a lot of fun that was enjoyed by all.

There are so many memories of Tech and the "after war" days that there is not enough space to mention them.

A very dear friend of mine, Bill Hashbarger, recently passed away. He and his wife Audie lived in the same trailer city and he often said to me, "Jock, when you were elected Mayor of our trailer city, it inspired me. When I retired from the Corps of Engineers I ran for Mayor of Russellville, and you know, I was elected." Bill was a wonderful friend and loved one.

Again, I would not take anything for my college days and the memories derived from being Mayor of that city and hearing the stories of all those who lived nearby.

*****

I could not continue my discussion about Tech without mentioning Coach John Tucker. Coach Tucker played football at the University of Alabama, in the same backfield with Johnny Mack Brown, the movie actor.

Coach Tucker was a disciplinarian of the first order. He was a total winner in every respect. He gave as much as he demanded from his players. When you visit the archives of football memorabilia in Tucker Auditorium, you will view row after row of trophies that are indicative of his leadership. Even Arkansas Tech University, in years past, played ARMY.

*****

Our President of the University, Dr. J. W. Hull, was the finest example of integrity I have ever known. Dr. Hull made it a point to know as many of the students by name as possible. It was nothing to meet Dr. Hull on campus and have him call you by your first name. He was one of the finest, with reference to politics, when he would visit the Legislature to help push through legislation that related to education. What a wonderful First Lady Mrs. Hull was. She, also, was an example of extraordinary integrity.

*****

STEPS TO SUCCESS

Just think, without the G.I. Bill I would have never entered college. I believe the readership of this story would relish a fact that I just found out while visiting Georgia recently. A friend of mine there, asked me this question, "Jock, do you know exactly how the G.I. Bill came about?" I replied, "No, but I would like to know."

His remarks were this, "When the G.I. Bill was voted on in the House of Representatives, it was hung with a tie vote. My friend's father-in-law, Rep. John S. Gibson, was summoned from his home in Georgia to come and vote. He traveled to D.C., voted 'yea' and that is why we were rewarded with the G.I. Bill.

This gentleman should be awarded some type of memorial because of the thousands of veterans who are enjoying the fruits of Mr. Gibson's labor.

E.C. O'Neil, Jock and Neil Jackson, Hall of Distinction Members, Arkansas Tech University

CHAPTER 13

KOREAN CONFLICT

Following World War II, my concentration was on getting a degree from an accredited college.

Well, about a year before I received my degree, a buddy of mine explained to me that by joining an Army Reserve unit and spending a little time at drill, I would draw drill pay, which I could use. This sounded very good and outside of summer camps in an Artillery unit at Fort Sill, Oklahoma in the summer, the drills weren't bad at all.

Well, after graduating from ATU and getting my first job as a teacher in middle school in Altus, Arkansas, I opened my mail one day. I was informed that I was to report to the Army and Navy Hospital in Hot Springs, Arkansas for a final type physical that would place me on active duty during the Korean Conflict. I had several buddies who had been called and with six weeks of training, they were off and running to the battlefield in North Korea.

Being newly married and loving my new-found profession made it really hard to leave it all and re-enter the military. I was to report to the Military District Headquarters in Little Rock for assignment. I traveled to the headquarters and reported to a Colonel there for a briefing and for him to try to place me in a position that I was suited for.

Well, the Colonel asked me if I had my degree and I said, "Yes." He asked me if I could type. I replied "Yes." He then asked how many words per minute? I replied, "105." Then the Colonel turned to me and said, "Son, how would you like to live here in Little Rock and serve this Headquarters?" After a courteous, "Yes, Sir," I knew then that I was in great shape.

I remained on duty in this Headquarters for about two and a half years, wearing my uniform during the day and civilian clothes the rest of the time. I was a softball "Fast Pitch" pitcher and pitched for the Headquarters and loved every minute of it.

About this time, my wife became pregnant and nine months later our daughter, "Jibby," was born.

I worked in the communications division of the Headquarters and worked with some of the best people in the world. I enjoyed my work very much.

As the Korean War came to an end, I was notified that my tenure of work had been completed and that I had to make a decision. I was told that I could stay in the army, be promoted to Second Lt. in the Adjutant General's Corps and go for a retirement when I reached the rank of Lt. Colonel.

There was one catch. I had a right inguinal hernia on the right side and could not be promoted until I had surgery and the hernia repaired. I decided to go for the surgery, even though I was sure that I was not staying in. I had the surgery at the Army and Navy hospital in Hot Springs and everything turned out fine.

Looking back, this was a very good decision because of the opportunities that the National Guard offered, but at that time the National Guard had not even entered my mind. I was given a honorable discharge, for the second time, and my wife and I moved back to Russellville.

I accepted a sales job, traveling northwest Arkansas.

One day while I was visiting with a good friend, a guardsman, Captain Troy Burris, he asked me if I would like to join the 217th Engineer Battalion as a 2nd Lt. and serve under him. I told him I would discuss the situation with my wife and let him know.

1st Sgt. Razz Lawrence standing with Captain Jock Davis

CHAPTER 14

THE NATIONAL GUARD

Upon being discharged as a 3rd Lt. after my service during the Korean War, I often wondered if I should become engaged in reserve forces duty such as the Army Reserves or the Army National Guard.

Well, my wonderment became a reality when Captain Troy Burris asked me if I would be interested in serving under him in Headquarters Company of the 217th Engineer Battalion, Russellville, Arkansas. After much thought and conversation with my wife, I decided to join.

The Battalion Headquarters was located in the Stroupe Building at Arkansas Tech University. The Battalion Commander was Lt. Col., Robert Young, and his office was housed in this building, along with the full-time and part-time staff.

My first assignment was that of platoon leader. Of course, it was not very long before I was promoted to lst Lt. and received a little more drill pay.

I can well remember in the spring of that year our convoy traveling from Russellville to

Little Rock and Camp Robinson for duty there on the firing range. It was during the month of April, and a cold front came through the state, with plenty of moisture. There was wind and storms, and did it ever turn cold. My driver and I were in a jeep, wide open, without side flaps and we could see ice hanging from the trees and all of the troops were cold because they were not prepared for it.

There are two other vivid memories that exist with that cold weather. One was that it was freezing cold, with a brisk breeze on the firing range, and the other was that I lost all of my azalea bushes that were crushed by the ice flow. Let me tell you, you do not lose azalea bushes unless it is bitter cold, and it was that.

At any rate, we fired for record, with the Battalion all in force, and had to drive back the next day, which was tolerable. We were able to stay warm in the hutments that were furnished for us.

*****

Our Battalion was made up of a Headquarters company, located in Russellville, a company in Dardanelle, a company in

Danville, a company in Clarksville and one in Morrilton.

The bridge platoons were the most interesting. Their duties were to lay the Bailey Bridge, a well known bridge at that time for Engineer units. I remember well one time while encamped at Fort Polk, Louisiana, that Lt. Bert Mullins, a platoon leader had his men on assignment, throwing a Bailey across a stream on the confines of Fort Polk.

After the bridge was completed, there was always a time to commend their unit for "A job well done!" This was celebrated by throwing one of the officers off into the water. Well, Lt. Mullins got lucky on that hot, August afternoon. He got dunked. Lt. Paul Pugh was another fellow officer who had the same assignment. He relished the opportunity of being dunked.

I believe one of the most satisfying times was to sit after chow in the evening and listen to our 1st Sergeant tell stories to the young men who had just joined the unit. This was done while on bivouac.

One of these stories, a story about an Armadillo still exists today. One night about midnight I saw one running through camp. I thought he looked different. One of our men had tied a helmet liner on his back and he was trying to shake it off. It was hilarious.

Normally our summer encampment lasted two weeks and that included convoy time from Russellville to Ft. Polk. One of my duties was to travel in and out of the convoy in a jeep, making sure each deuce and a half had the proper distance.

One day, my driver, 1st Sergeant Razz Lawrence and I were cruising along, driving in and out of the convoy when we noticed a trailer pulled behind a jeep, its tires almost flat. We pulled the jeep over. I crawled out of my jeep, went over to the driver and said, "Did you know your tires are almost flat?" He said, "Yes Sir!" I asked, "What is in the trailer?" He said, "Oh just some stuff."

This did not satisfy me, so I walked around the back of the trailer, lifted up the cover and there were masses of cans of beer, all iced down. In order to not make a rhubarb over the findings, I got back in my jeep and Razz and I drove away. I found out later that they had the beer to sell during bivouac to their people. No one ever knew of this instance except Razz and I.

$$*****$$

Let me tell you a bit about Razz. He was one of the finest 1st Sergeants I have ever been associated with. His men loved him dearly, would have died for him. He had the best discipline out of his men than any enlisted man that I have ever seen.

I can remember the time when I was elevated to Company Commander. I called Razz into my office. He entered with the appropriate salute and sat in front of me. I was relaxed with my chair reared back with my boots upon my desk. I commenced to tell Razz what I expected from him. In fact I told him that if I ever had to take my boots off the top of my desk due to some foul up with the enlisted personnel, that they would be, YOU KNOW WHERE. I never had to take my boots off my desk.

Razz was a tremendous athlete in high school. He was a man's man and would do anything possible for his men.

I do remember one time that he was embarrassed. We were in Garrison, in Barracks at Ft. Polk. As you might expect, Col. Young expected cleanliness along with orderliness. One morning, Major Troy Burris, now

Executive Officer of the Battalion reporting to Colonel Young, called me, as Company Commander, to see if I was ready for the mess hall to be inspected. I immediately said, "Yes Sir." Major Burris said he would be right over.

Well, before Major Burris had called, I had asked Razz if the mess hall was ready for inspection? He immediately responded, "Yes Sir!" Well, in about five minutes, I saluted Major Burris and with Razz in tow, we walked to the mess hall. I opened the back door to the mess hall, looked in and there was a wad of mop fuzz balled up, lying on the drain in the middle of the floor.

Major Burris saw it at the same time and said, "Captain Davis, are you sure you are ready for inspection." I replied, "No sir, but I will call you when I am ready, if that would be alright?"

When Sergeant Razz had been dressed down and I knew for sure the mess had been picked up, I called Major Burris, he came down and we passed the inspection with flying colors.

There were so many comical things that happened at summer camp that there are not enough pages to list them all.

Most of our Battalion were made up of ex-service men, most of them serving during WWII and the Korean Conflict. You can imagine the vast experience back then that existed among the ranks.

If that Battalion had been called to Active Duty today to either Afghanistan or Iraq, experience would have taken over. This does not mean that our National Guard units today are not ready. It just means that these men had been fighting two wars and knew the story and drill.

*****

My good buddy Lt. Bert Mullens (now a banker), was a Bridge Platoon leader, who was always wanting to have a little fun. There was little fun to be had with the temperature at 100 degrees and no breeze during summer encampment at Camp Joseph T. Robinson, near Little Rock.

After a hard days work of training, throwing the Bailey Bridge, a task of which Bert was very astute, he called me on the field phone and said, "Davis, do you want to have a little fun?" I answered, "Why not?" Then he said, "I have one of the assault boats that we rest our bridge on and I would like to go down to supply, draw an outboard motor and take the little boat for a spin." I said, "OK," and I was on my way to the lake, not far from where he had been "throwing the Bailey."

Bert choked the motor, then pulled the cord and the motor started. The boat leveled out and we were enjoying a nice ride around the lake when lo and behold there was a large bump sound, we looked at the back of the boat and there was no motor. Well, not being fishermen, we never thought about placing a safety chain from the motor to the boat.

"Oh my goodness," Bert said, "Capt. Burris is going to be very unhappy about this." Seeing as how he would have to sign a statement of charges and be charged about $500 for this motor. Bert said to me in a very alarmed voice, "What do we do now?" and I said, "There is not but one thing to do and that is go to Capt. Burris, tell him our story and maybe he will understand."

Well, knowing Capt. Burris, he would care less and would ream us out. We went to the mess hall and hailed Capt. Burris. We told him of our plight and his response was, "Well, Lt., you know where the motor is and I suggest you have that motor out of the water by night or you two will be in hot water." We replied, "Yes Sir."

We sat down and pondered on what we could do. All of a sudden I had this great idea. We had one of our enlisted men by the name of Willie T. Smith who was a perfect diver and swimmer and we would contact him and see if he could help us out.

We hunted until we found Willie T. and asked him if he could help us. He offered his services and we were off and running to try to find the motor. We paddled out to the spot where we thought the motor was, tied a rope around Willie T's waist and let him down in about six feet of water.

Shortly after his dive, he came to the surface and said, "I found the motor." We immediately gave him another rope, he dived again, tied off the motor with the rope and surfaced. We pulled up the motor, delivered it to the supply shop where they cleaned and oiled it. Capt. Burris was happy and that was the happy ending.

There was another incident I will never forget that was funny, also about my good friend and college classmate, 1st Lt. Bert Mullens. He and I were standing along our jeeps awaiting orders to pull out to the field for bivouac, when, unknown to Mullens, a hand patted him on the back and said, "Lt. I have my pot on (meaning helmet liner) and you should have yours on." Looking very pale and surprised, Lt. Mullens snapped to attention and said, "Sir, it is on my head and I sure am sorry."

It was General Trousdale.

*****

I will never forget those hot, sweltering nights in the field, waiting until two o'clock in the morning, when the cool would set in and you could sleep three or four hours.

I also remember a time when we had gotten our packs and pup tents off of our truck, and started setting up our small area of encampment underneath a large group of oak trees. I remember that Lt. Mullens, Capt. Tom Wilson, our Chaplain, Warrant Officer Watson and Sgt. Patterson were all within a stone's throw of each other.

Just as we got settled in, I looked up the road and there came Major Troy Burris. Major Burris waited until he got almost up to our encampment area and yelled as loud as he could,

"March Order." It was seven o'clock in the evening, we were tired and now the Colonel had given Major Burris an order to tell everyone to pull up stakes and we were to convoy to another area. Well, it seemed that with one gasp Sgt. Patterson pulled out his entrenching tool, threw it into the ground and yelled a bad word. The Chaplain, in disdain as we all were, said, "Endorsement."

*****

Keep in mind that there were twenty years of these summer visits to Polk.

I suppose if there was anything I tolerated during this time it was the field encampment. We would convoy into the field and each Company would camouflage their weapons and trucks and we would be there for five days.

I remember a story that Dr. Harris, a Major, and our Battalion Doctor, told us. He had been to a Divisional meeting, early on, for a briefing about things you should and should not do during encampment.

During the meeting, Dr. Harris was asked, "Doc, what about these poisonous snakes while we are in the field." "Well," Doc said, "There is one snake that does not strike, it chews on your ear lobe, your nose or wherever it can hold on."

The young man, still inquisitive, asked, "Doc, do you ever die from this bite?" Doc replied, "Well, another doctor said during the meeting that they had a soldier get drunk and tried to kiss this snake and when he did, the snake bit him and he was dead before he could get his tongue back in his mouth." The man said in a very soft voice, "Really?"

Everyone laughed and even though Doc Harris has passed on, this story is a good one and is still being used during our reunions.

*****

How well I remember those long winded politicians from Arkansas and Louisiana who would stand on that platform, while we troops were standing "At Ease", and deliver their messages. Keep in mind that the temperature was 100 degrees Fahrenheit and no shade. When the speaking was over, the band started and we would parade in review past the review stand. There was not a dry thread on any of us at the close of the parade.

I will never forget a bright and sunny afternoon on the parade field at Camp Polk where our Battalion would stand in ranks and listen to repeated speeches by the Governor of Arkansas, Governor of Louisiana and General Trousdale, Camp Commander from the Guard in Louisiana. The temperature being 105 degrees with no breeze and listening to these gentlemen extol their exploits politically, I must say that our medics did a good job of keeping our boys and others safe after they would pass out from the heat. They would have to "litter carry" them off of the Parade Field.

I remember one parade in particular when a good friend of mine, Captain Mule Presley ,said, "Davis, if I pass out, let me lay there and if a medic tries to haul me off I will scream and kick my way to heaven."

I also remember well as a 1st Lt. at another parade at Fort Chaffee, Arkansas, suffering a feeling of embarrassment for myself. After the parade, our Governor of the state, Governor Dale Bumpers, came up to me and said, "Davis, it is real good to see you." I stood at attention and said, "Sir, it is very good to see you, sir." After the parade I was telling one of my fellow officers that I wondered how the Governor knew my name and he remarked, "I suppose he read your name tag." As I said, a time of embarrassment.

*****

Another memorable moment was when I had arrived back home, my wife was unpacking my duffel bag and a spike-heeled ladies golden slipper hit the floor and she was on it like a dog on a bone.

I tried to explain how the shoe got there, which was sometime during the time I was in the shower the evening before we left for home. Someone, and I know who, slipped the golden slipper in my duffel bag and closed it.

Well, while I was in the process of explaining to my wife, I received a call and the caller asked to speak to my wife. It was Mr. Melvern Watson, one of our warrant officers who knew exactly the time I needed him to call. He explained that he was the culprit who had hidden the shoe. All was well and my buddy had saved my life.

There is no telling how many duffel bags that shoe had made its way into in twenty to thirty years.

*****

Our S-4 section, under the guidance of Major Hartzel Bartlett, did a magnificent job of purifying water out of an old slough and making it crystal clear, drinkable and useable for showers.

I must tell you that this section did a marvelous job of supplying great food for our cooks to use while in the field and in Garrison. I believe my favorite was the southern fried chicken with apple cobbler for dessert.

Sergeants Motley and Bewley, both deceased, did a remarkable job of keeping us fed.

*****

As I mentioned earlier, from the time I was ten years of age, which was 1934, until the Central High Crisis, we four boys were constantly taught not to play with the colored people in colored town.

During the Central High situation our Battalion was called to active duty. We were instructed to report to the armory early each morning, answer roll call, and get the readings of the day. We were informed if any of us were to report to Little Rock, and if we were not, we could go about our merry way to work and report back the next morning for roll call. Several of our men were called to Little Rock but I was never called.

Our duty would be to protect and defend the black students who wanted to attend Central High.

Occasionally, some of my buddies who were activated would recount activities and we would discuss it lightly.

Many of my best friends today are black and I am thankful for them. I cannot help but remember the animosity that my mom had toward the black people. I suppose she took these feelings to the grave. It was how she was reared and she never grew out of those feelings.

Of course the black area of town wasn't too far from our house and sometimes I would just accidentally happen into their neighborhood without knowing it. They had their own schools, their own football team and actually, not much for uniforms. They did, however, have pride in their teams and their schools, even though there was little money to operate on.

You know that during those depression

years, the whites had very little, so you can imagine what the black settlements had.

I can remember on the ship overseas during WWII, loaded with 600 troops, the blacks were housed in the bottom holds of the ship and the whites were housed on all the decks all the way to the top. This was in early 1944. In February of 46, on my way back on a troop ship from Manila, there was a black man sleeping above me in his hammock.

Another instance of the change since 1944 was the way we were housed in tents awaiting our ships to come home when we had points. Blacks were in the same tents with whites. When their names appeared on the bulletin boards, they would be transported to the same area and slept on cots next to the whites. This, I knew, was a good sign of things to come. Yes, desegregation was on it's way.

Today, there has been a huge awakening on both sides, but, I can see we still have a long way to go. The thing I do not understand is why this turmoil of a few students wanting to attend high school was thwarted by then Governor Orval Faubus.

Not many persons are still left alive who can recall many instances of the race turmoil that I felt as a young man in South Arkansas. The very idea of white men in sheets, scaring the daylights out of dark people is sad. At some point in time, those who have enacted these terrible acts will have to account for them.

There will be a recounting of these awful deeds in heaven and many questions will be asked such as "Why did you treat my people that way?" Then they will have to answer. Only our God has the authority to punish those misdeeds.

*****

To this day the 217th Engineer Battalion, the 217th Maintenance Battalion, and the 206th Artillery Battalion conduct a homecoming every two or three years at the armory to love up our buddies, talk over old times and extol the past.

And I began to climb the ladder of Military success by being promoted to 1st Lt. as Executive Officer to Capt. Burris. Then, it seems in a very short time I was promoted to Company Commander, a Captain and Capt.

Burris was promoted to Major and the Battalion Commander's Executive Officer.

I served in this capacity for several years and my time was closing in to be promoted to Major but there was no vacancy. I heard that the Adjutant General, General Tom Phillips, was developing a new unit, the 176 P.A.D., which stood for Public Affairs Detachment. This Commander, a Major, reported directly to the Adjutant General and the unit was located at Camp Robinson, in Little Rock, Arkansas.

I was very excited to have this opportunity. I was asked to be interviewed by General Phillips. The interview went well and I was offered the job which I readily accepted.

Our job was to cover the AG (Adjutant General) in all facets of his work. We had approximately 15 very professional cameramen, writers and journalism experts on our staff. Capt. Bill Lawson was my executive officer and he did his job well. There were two other officers and the rest were enlisted personnel who shot the cameras, did press releases, handled the dark room and released a periodic newspaper.

This probably was one of the closest knit units I have ever served with. Our people loved each other and covered each other when a news worthy item would break. Cissy Coleman was a bright spark in the unit, always having something going. Cissy became, later on, a commissioned officer, a helicopter pilot and commanded the aviation department and I believe retired as a Colonel. It was an extreme pleasure to serve as her commander.

Summer camps, especially at Fort Chaffee, Arkansas, were a lot of fun for our troops because our people had to cover several thousands of troops who did their summer encampments there.

We covered the influx of Cuban people, the Vietnam aliens who arrived at Chaffee and many more nationalities who spent time at Chaffee before being placed in the United States. I suppose today the reason for the influx of foreigners into the United States was influenced by the Fort Chaffee numbers who came here after Korea, Vietnam and Cuba.

Being the commander of the 176 PAD gave me the opportunity to manage my detachment of fully qualified journalism graduates which, at the time, were mostly single and caught the eyes of the young Cuban, Vietnamese, and Korean ladies who were placed in the Chaffee compound. Their duties were not to mingle with the cordoned off areas of these people, but rather take pictures and write the stories that related to our troops in policing these areas for two weeks. This was our encampment for the summer.

There will always be a dear spot in my heart for Fort Chaffee, for it was the camp from which I departed for during World War II. Little did I know at the time I was separated there I would some day spend time as a Guardsman, keeping watch over these people who had been displaced.

Of course, again with the huge hurricane that hit New Orleans, there was a need for Fort Chaffee again to handle these displaced persons.

The two-story, World War II barracks again came in handy for their placements. The duration of stay for these people was not long at all. Many of them were given refuge in hotels, camps and other lodging, after moving them from Fort Chaffee.

Today, Fort Chaffee is a training area for the Arkansas National Guard and I understand that it is being used part of the year for the Seals training program by the Federal Government.

Well, with this all said, many of the two-story barracks burned to the ground, with only the furnace stacks still standing. There was a controlled burn being done, as I understand it, and a very high wind came up and consumed many of the barracks. Even though the barracks along state Hwy. 22 were burned, there are many of these two-story barracks still standing.

I have attended many camps in my thirty-seven plus years of service, but Chaffee is still the one that is dear to my heart.

*****

Little did I know that, with the pay from drills and summer camps, I would be able to pay for the education of our daughter at Ouachita Baptist University. Little did I know that my retirement income as a Major would far exceed my expectations. Those thirty-seven years were memorable ones and the relationship with my men will remain with me until I depart this world.

Above: Jock as grand marshal at a Veteran's Day parade in Russellville.
Below: Jock greets then-Governor David Pryor at National Guard Camp.

PART 3

MY PROFESSIONAL
AND
COMMUNITY SERVICE
YEARS

CHAPTER 15

MY DEVELOPMENT AND TRAINING YEARS

During my fifty or so years in Agri-Business, I had the opportunity to work with Land Grant Colleges in recruiting and eventually in seminar teaching. Some of those Universities were: Texas A&M, University of Arkansas, Auburn University, University of Georgia, Mississippi State University and some work with the University of Kansas.

In recruiting for the Poultry Industry, I was constantly on watch for a young man or lady who possessed management skills that would send them to the front of the line in Poultry Top Management. Today, I can proudly say that there are many at the top with six-figure salaries pushing them forward.

Always, when I would visit a university to make a pitch to the graduating seniors, I made a prior appointment with the head of the department concerning my company. The next morning I would commence my interviews. One thing I noticed when addressing these seniors was, when I would make the request,

"Let me see the hands of those who know exactly what they would like to do when they graduate." Only five percent raised their hands. I found this to be the case wherever I traveled.

Back in the 50's and 60's there were no power points so I had to make do with flip charts and slide paraphernalia that traveled with me. At any rate, I got the job done.

I suppose my particular "Pick of the litter" was Mississippi State University. First of all, I was enthralled with the work ethic of these undergraduate students. At night you never saw them down town spending time and money that they did not have. They were either working at a job or in their room studying. I love that work ethic.

Of course, State always had everything at my disposal coming into the interview. Students were always on time and dressed neatly and well read on "Interviewing Techniques." Many of those young, starry-eyed graduates grace the top side of our industry today.

Dr. Wallace Morgan, head of the Poultry Science Department at Mississippi State, was and is my best friend still today.

One day while we were conversing over a game of golf, Wallace asked about a seminar that a colleague and I had devised for TastyBird Foods.

A fellow personnel employee of TastyBird by the name of Jack Clack and I devised this seminar for middle and upper management personnel of the company, upon the request of the President, Mr. Don Dalton. Don had noticed management personnel pulling apart from the team and wanted something to repair it.

So, Jack and I devised the acronym G.Y.S.T., which stood for GET YOUR STUFF TOGETHER! with handbooks, case studies and role play. We then took the team of eight managers to a resort in Missouri to hold them captive for three days and nights. To make a long story short, Mr. Dalton came up on the final night, had dinner with his managers, and listened to testimony from each manager concerning the seminar.

He was amazed that there was so much emotion and pulling together as a team, from this group, who in essence had been at each other's throat. He heard words like togetherness, love, caring, compassion, graciousness, etc. Well, that was the beginning of a successful seminar venture that has stayed intact for thirty-one years.

Dr. Morgan wanted to know all about this program so I sat down, gave him all the titled messages involved and their time frames, and he said, "I want you to present this program to our graduating seniors."

That was the beginning of a program that has gone on for over twenty-five years and is very successful in teaching our young people the "Facts of Life", that include commitment and integrity.

I estimate that over two thousand persons have gone through this program. The main thrust that sets this seminar apart from others is "The Love Syndrome!" We can hardly get ahead in life unless we help those less fortunate.

In getting into the Love Syndrome, at the conclusion of each seminar I address the word "love" and what it should mean to all of us.

In doing so, I present them with an Eisenhower silver dollar that carries the printed name, "Love Wheel."

Many times I have visited with persons who have gone through the course years before and they show me the silver dollar, with the sides worn slick and they always say, "I love you." They know in my heart that I care for them deeply and they return the favor. What a blessing this course meant to my life.

After Jack Clack left TastyBird and I retired for the first time, I decided to patent the idea, GYST, and today I am still teaching this idea at Mississippi State, church surroundings and other groups who are interested in the program.

Just a word about my friend, Dr. Wallace Morgan; he was always there for me, asking me if he could help in any way, and he always had the kids jacked up ready for my call.

He and his wife, Mary Martha, live in Starkville in a beautiful rural setting and Wallace spends many retirement hours in his wood shop doing all sorts of fine work with wood. I have in my possession a beautiful cedar bowl that he made just for me and autographed on the bottom side. I have this bowl sitting in a visible space in my office where it is truly a conversation piece.

Those thirty or so years that we conversed by phone before the advent of computer were years that I will always honor as being his friend.

I would be remiss if I did not mention our days on the golf course. Wallace, until he had several surgeries, could hit the ball long and straight. After we played eighteen, he would always say, "Go ahead and give me a George

Washington so I can frame it." I would naturally fork over a one dollar bill. I have never had as good a time playing golf with anyone as I did with Wallace.

Dr. Wallace Morgan was always there for his students. If he wasn't teaching them the virtues of life, he was teaching them that "To expect more is to get more!" He always kept up with his graduating seniors. Whether they would go on to be a Vet or a first line supervisor, he always taught them to enjoy life and in doing that, to help someone else. Oh, how his students loved him and love him still today.

Jock stands in the middle holding a plaque in honor of his many years of service to Mississippi State Poultry Science. Dr. Morgan stands to the far left

CHAPTER 16

G.Y.S.T:
"GET YOUR SELF TOGETHER"

In all my training years, there is no other relic that I treasure more than my handbook that translates into success.

Over 2,000 young leaders have enjoyed the process of training that included not only training for future management success but the activities associated with the many courses.

As I mentioned earlier, at the conclusion of each three day session, I presented each member of the class a Silver Dollar as a gift of love, which we called the "Love Wheel" and asked them to carry this with them to be reminded that they should tell someone during the day that they love them. Along with the coin went a frameable, 8 1/2 X 11 printed sheet to remind them of some of the words that dictate love.

Many years after a person had received their wheel and I would see them on the processing line, they would pull out the coin, with both tails and heads worn off, and say, "I do remember and I do love you."

This was well worth the time spent extolling

each member of the class to try to achieve success in their life to come. I had hoped to include a copy of this manual with this book, but it just wasn't practical as we neared publication.

Also, there is a sixteen page booklet on "Discipline" that you can follow as you continue life in this business related society. Both of these manuals are available from me upon request.

I have seen many evidences of young people who have put these books to practice and are very successful today. It is my hope they do the same for you.

Also, I do hope that everyone who reads this book takes the time to sit down and write a summary of their outlook on life. You won't regret it.

I recently had the wonderful opportunity to visit Mississippi to conduct a three-day GYST seminar to Poultry Science Students. What a pleasure it was to introduce myself and have them to do the same, and explore their faces with looks that were worth a thousand words.

I know deep in my inner self that they wondered what this guy could say that would make them love his words and presentation on such a beautiful day.

Well, at the conclusion of the course and after listening to their remarks about the course, I was well satisfied with the work that I had done.

Remember, many of these students will be going out in life to seek their fortune. In my heart I knew that I had left an impression that I loved them and wanted them to succeed in life.

After the day was over, I suggested that we go the local Country Club for eighteen holes of golf. Most of them had never touched a golf club, much less been on a golf course.

Well, Dr. Morgan had arranged for golf carts, fees and all that went with it. That is just the way he is.

We crawled into the carts and were off for an afternoon of laughing, hitting balls into trees and water and all types of antics for a group who has never hit a golf ball. Man, it was fun and was an afternoon that I will never forget. Of course, I had to fork over another dollar bill to Dr. Morgan.

I suppose several things stand out while teaching these kids. The big thing is to get them to commit and sign a commitment card that says they can do 15% more in a days work. They had never thought about such a commitment.

The next thing is listening to their presentations. Each student is given an assignment to present a stand-up presentation, using a flip-chart, to sell someone on an idea or program, handle confrontation, make a speech and be able to sell me, as the buyer, within fifteen minutes.

Most of them had never heard of the "illumination technique." To "illumine" someone is to brag on them.

Another highlight was getting them interested in two subjects: commitment and integrity. Using my handbook and breaking into share groups, they discussed case studies and brought their findings to the rest of the class.

Many students are scared to death to go before their peers and make a presentation. On top of this, finding out, truly, what commitment and integrity really means to them and their future made the class much more palatable.

After the presentations, each person is given the opportunity to share with the professor or myself what they have learned during the past three days. I have never heard a bad remark, unless it was that the class was not long enough.

Upon presentation of their plaques, I did a thirty-minute presentation on the "Love Syndrome of Life." This presentation included handing out the printed Love Wheel to each person as well as an Eisenhower silver dollar that signified my love for them and truly was the Love Wheel. I asked them to do one thing for me: Love was given to them. Now pass it on.

I only wish those of you who are reading this book could enjoy one of my classes. Surely in my 86 years of life, and 60 out of that in selling and managing people, I have planted seeds that all my students can grow in life.

All of these modules were written by myself or Jack Clack. There have been over 2,000, pre-management types, middle managers and college graduates, who have gone through this three-day course.

The training started with a dinner the evening before, at a resort or place that took the students from their work environment to the restful resort area.

Classes started at 8:00 A.M. the next morning after breakfast and concluded at noon that day. After lunch, each student was required to enter into some type of competition that had a team setting, such as golf, tennis, or bike riding, etc.

This program concluded on the third day of the seminar with a banquet dinner. The president of the company, or department head, if it was a college, was invited to the banquet.

Each student was asked to rise and recite their feelings about the seminar. I must say that I never heard a derogatory story concerning the seminar. Awards were presented to all the students and that concluded the seminar.

In closing this chapter on GYST, I would share with you as I have with over 2,000 former students: If you will help others get what they want in life you will never want for your desires in life. This is so true.

CHAPTER 17

A LIFETIME OF SELLING

After fifty-five years of selling, I find myself selling more than I ever did when I was being paid for it. We ALL sell everyday of our life without even knowing it. It may include selling your wife or family on something you would like to do. It might be selling an idea to one of your golfing partners, or it might be a volunteer program that you would like for others to enter into.

Intangible selling is that selling of an item you cannot see or feel. This is sometimes tough, sometimes easy, considering what the idea or program is. For instance, calling friends for a donation for the American Cancer Society. This is not a hard one to sell because we have all been touched one way or the other with this dreaded disease.

At any rate, we are all sales people, out there pounding the pavement to sell a product or idea.

When I received my degree from Arkansas Tech University, the first thing I wanted to do was to find a job. I was interviewed and hired as a sixth grade teacher and assistant basketball coach at the Altus, AR school system. It was at the beginning of the Korean War and teachers were hard to find.

I made it through over half of one semester and lo and behold I was called back into the service of my country.

Upon being discharged as a Second Lt., at the end of the war, I was interviewed by General Mills, Feed Division, as a sales person. This was a wonderful company with many benefits. Unfortunately, this Feed Division no longer exists due to many thousands of turkeys needing to be disposed of after having come in contact with a product used on the range to kill chiggers. These turkeys were being fed on open range and this great loss of feed and the costs to feed these big birds caused General Mills to leave the feed industry.

Today they are still a large factor in cereals and other products. I was then hired by Central Soya Company, as a sales person and manager to cover an area in Northwest Arkansas.

During my seven years with Soya, I maintained a level of the top salesmen over the United States and, in 1966, I became a member of the prestigious Wildcat Club of the company. Out of approximately 350 salesmen, I was the top tonnage salesman the year before. We were flown to Miami Beach, Florida, with all the salesmen in attendance, and then awarded the Wildcat Award. This was one of the highlights of my life, to stand before my peers and be recognized as one of their top sales people.

In 1978, I was contacted by Don Dalton, President of Valmac Industries, and asked to join his staff as Director of Development and Training. My duties included making all staff meetings, keeping the president abreast of training, attitudes and program development involved in the company. One of my duties was to edit a newsletter that came out each month that was packed full of stories about the growers, employees and anyone else who made Valmac tick.

Don probably had the best management style of anyone I have ever worked for. He was a man of few words and, as the saying used to go, "When Don smiled, he was tickled to death."

In 1984, I decided to retire. Almost at the exact time, Tyson Foods purchased TastyBird Foods, whose predecessor was Valmac. Blake Lovette was president.

There is just so much golfing, church work and volunteerism you can do and be happy. Not long after I retired, a good friend, once associated with Tastybird, contacted me and asked if I would be interested in working with O.K. Feeds and reporting to him as Assistant to the President. I talked it over with my wife and started driving to Ft. Smith, Arkansas, to work three days per week.

This is one of those jobs that if you don't like any facet of it, you can quit at any time and be happy about it. Anyway, I started a job then that would last over ten years.

Mike Pruitt, O.K. Feeds President, knew of the management program called GYST. He asked me to take every supervisor through the program and even write an intermediate and advanced course for the program, which I did.

Some of the programs taught were: Discipline in Industry, Selling Techniques, Leadership Styles, Setting and Reaching Goals, Team Building, and many more, too numerous to mention.

Before long, word was out that everyone was gaining much from the training and I was asked to take it throughout the company which, at that time, encompassed approximately 1,500 to 2,000 supervisory personnel. These training seminars were held at resort areas to get the employees away from the work environment. Normally, the course concluded after three days of training, and on the final evening, Mike was flown in for an awards ceremony and given the opportunity to hear testimony from those present about the program.

At the age of 86, I am still teaching one or more times yearly in the Poultry Science Department at Mississippi State University. I have either taught or recruited at MSU for over thirty-one years.

Now as I said earlier, my association with Dr. Wallace Morgan, now retired as the Professor and Head of the Poultry Science Department, has been so pleasant, in fact, I consider him to be one of the best friends I have ever had. He should be an example to all other heads of colleges and universities of whom I would like to lead my child into life after graduation. Dr. Morgan gave his all for the University and every kid who graduated from the Poultry Science Department.

CHAPTER 18

CHICKENS BEFORE VERTICAL INTEGRATION

First of all, I will try to explain the definition of Vertical Integration in the Poultry Industry. Vertical Integration is the integration of all facets into a Poultry Company or Complex.

The needs included: a feed mill, a hatchery, breeder hens to lay the eggs for broiler chicks, and finally a marketing department to market the chicks.

Included in this were rolling stock such as, bulk feed trucks, trucks with cages to bring the birds into the plant and a contract with grain companies to supply protein and grain as a diet for the birds to bring them into maturity for slaughter and processing.

Before that time, normally a feed company was responsible for selling a farmer on building a poultry house, which normally would house 500 to 1,000 birds. Grower contracts were not prevalent in the early 50's so more than likely a handshake did the job.

In those days, a feed dealer would hunt high and low for baby chicks to fill the houses, order feed from a reputable feed company and then do the best job possible to locate a processing plant that would buy the birds for processing.

Placing birds in those days was dramatically different than it is today. Rings of corrugated cardboard, about 12 inches in height were laid on the ground and were about six feet in width. Fountains for water were nothing but a quart fruit jar turned upside down in a water holder for them to drink out of. Water troughs, in about six foot lengths, were drawn to the ceiling with a pulley. Corrugated feeder lids with two inch lips on them were placed in the pens to pour crumbled feed in to start the chicks on.

When the birds were two weeks old, the water troughs would be lowered to the height of the chickens. To clean a trough, a short handled mop was used to wash the trough daily by using disinfectant.

Because of no breeding history, the birds were very thin breasted and the thighs and drums were small. The high energy feed that we use today was not prevalent during that feeding time, therefore the grow out period was about eight to ten weeks.

In those days, a tractor trailer rig would drive miles delivering the birds to the closest processing plant for processing. You can imagine the time and loss during a day when the temperature was near 100 degrees.

Now, just a word about the historical names that I have been honored to sit in meetings with. During the fifties, there was a man by the name of Harold Snyder who had the vision to build a feed mill on the bank of the Arkansas River near Dardanelle, Arkansas. Harold was a Vocational Agricultural teacher at the Dardanelle High School and mixed poultry feeds on the floor of the Agri building. I suppose this huge movement by this man laid the ground work for Vertical Integration.

Ed Harms, Charles Boyce and myself were employed by General Mills as salesmen. We were told that each Monday our assignments would be meted out by Mr. Snyder. Our job was to sell feed, due to the contract General Mills had with Mr. Snyder. This selling included getting farmers to build chicken houses and servicing the birds after they were placed.

At that time, we had no knowledge of diseases that would invade these chickens, the main culprit being bronchitis. I can remember well our team hearing about a new product to pour into the water troughs called Hadacol.

Some gentleman in Louisiana had developed this product, which included alcohol and it worked well on people, so why not use it on chickens? At this writing, I cannot tell you if it worked or not but it was the best that we had.

Harold Snyder was a very intelligent person. He came up with the idea that the heads of these small companies should meet at a specified time to have dinner, discuss the latest in poultry and then set another date to meet.

Our meeting place was the Pearson Hotel, now the 500 Building in Russellville, Arkansas. I can recall seeing each of these persons at the tables eating dinner and then gathering as a group to discuss prices, feed, medication, shipping, etc.

They were: Harold Snyder, Mr. John Tyson Sr., Mr. Gene George, Mr. Bill Simmons, Mr. Red Hudson and one or two more gentlemen, plus we three salesmen.

When you look at the businesses these men fathered and their offspring, who are managing them today, you think, "Man, was I in high cotton." Many of these have gone on to be with their Maker but you still see the trucks with signage that still silently says, "We sell chicken."

These mountains of businesses that is the number one industry in Arkansas started as small individual businesses and have grown into giants, all of them having the latest in hatchery, feed mills, processing and marketing.

We cannot forget the Allied Industries, including equipment companies that provide the state of the art in processing and feed manufacturing.

I would be remiss if I did not mention the giant breeder companies that have come so far in bringing a bird that is presentable to the consumer. Our country and especially our state is fortunate to have such fine companies that deliver these fine breeders and breeder eggs all over the world.

Cobb, Peterson, Hubbard are just a few that excel in this production.

I am old enough to remember the past and have reviewed the future when it comes to broiler production and to have known those giants in our industry who have made it happen is miraculous. Of course, when I'm considered a member of that august body of "The Greatest Generation," it swells me with pride that I have witnessed all of these wonderful happenings in technology, especially the Poultry Industry.

*****

TURKEYS - PAST AND PRESENT

Turkeys are another facet of our great industry that has had a tremendous makeover in the past sixty years. Dr. J.N. Thompson of Pottsville, Arkansas, long passed away, was partly responsible in transforming the color of this mighty bird.

I understand that Dr. Thompson received his Doctorate from Texas A & M and, after that, through several companies in poultry, helped transform this part of the industry with breeding.

For years the bird was a bronze color. During processing, it was found that pin feathers and other color pigmentation left the skin, discolored. It was decided that something must be done to correct this as it seemed to be a problem. Well, Dr. Thompson, along with others, set to work correcting this with turning the color of this mighty bird from bronze to white, which is what it is today.

While there was a transformation going on with medications, feeds, and most of all breeding, there was much work to be done.

One of the facets of my work as a salesman

for Central Soya was to service birds when they were sick, find a processor for them and get the best market possible for the sale of these birds.

One of the problems in growing these early birds was many of the large toms, when they would mature, would get excited over a predator, while out on the free range, and then die with a heart attack.

Through breeding, adjustment in feed and other factors, this was overcome. Today there is no free range of turkeys. The fencing is gone and replaced by huge poultry houses that confine the birds from start to market.

Dr. Thompson was so refined in his study of poultry that in the early years, he owned a hatchery and sold baby chicks to the local growers.

Along with this, I have seen jungle birds that Dr. Thompson shipped to his farm in Pottsville that he used in breeding up the birds.

*****

Concerning integrity and commitment: If parents do nothing else, they need to drill into their children that their word is their bond and if they tell someone they will do something then

164

they simply do it.

I called on the Agricultural Community for over fifty-five years and I can safely tell you that I always kept my word. If I made a commitment that I would be there to see them at a certain time, I made it a policy to be there at least fifteen to thirty minutes early.

You would be surprised how many times I got in early and how many times I made the sale.

Just because my three brothers and I grew up in a poor family setting, it did not mean that I was not clean inside and outside.

In my GYST teaching, integrity and commitment are two topics I spend at least two hours on doing case studies and role play.

It is so easy to tell the truth instead of lie. To tell the truth, you will never have to go back and cover it up with a lie. This principle is is so true when it comes to integrity and commitment.

CHAPTER 19

VOLUNTEERING IS GOOD

During the Depression years the word volunteer was not in the vocabulary of anyone. In fact, if you volunteered to help your mom or dad during those days, that was a feat.

Today, most psychiatrists will tell you that the two main ingredients for happiness is Love and Volunteerism. Of course, if you are a Christian and are in the Word, loving yourself is most important, why? Because your body is a temple, freely given to you by God. Naturally, the next step is loving your fellow man.

John 3:16 says, "For God so loved the world that he gave His only begotten Son that whosoever believes in Him would not perish but have everlasting life."

With this said, I would like to share with you my years of volunteer work and the aftermath of each and the results there derived.

After graduating from college and finishing my duty to my country, I entered the work force as a sales person. Being in sales does, or did then, give you a latitude to do things other than selling.

Being a member of First Baptist Church and trying to attend regularly, there was always someone there asking you to volunteer to do this or that. My first venture was that of a junior high Sunday School teacher.

If you have ever taught, you know that you must be prepared by study yourself. Even though the teacher was given a quarterly to go by, each student had the same lesson in their possession. Being there on time was a chore. This required getting seating ready, pencils on hand, and acquiring scratch paper. The next area was that of meeting the kids at the door and welcoming them.

Prayer at the beginning of class and at the close was necessary. If you have never taught children who are from 12 to 15 years of age, you would be surprised at how they test you to see if you are prepared. Questions of all types that related to the lesson that day were asked. I would usually pitch a question or two to the class for discussion. You would be surprised at the sound answers that came out of the mouths of these youth.

Of course, Sunday School was not the only function. There were also events such as wiener roasts, parties at their homes, hay rides and the likes. Sunday School teaching, if properly done, can be very time consuming.

The rewards are the memories of those early days. In fact, now, at the age of 86, I play golf with one of those boys, who is now a grandfather, nearly every week on John Daly's course. We have a great time together and when we come in contact with some friends on the course, Terry Dunn must tell them that I taught him in Sunday School and that I was a good one. Well, this made this volunteer effort a wonderful experience.

About three years later, I was asked to be Sunday School Superintendent for the same age group which included three teachers, most of them ladies. This was a very pleasant and less time consuming job. Before we broke into individual classes, we had a meeting of all the students and teachers to have a prayer time, talk about upcoming parties, etc.

This job lasted for about another three years and then I joined an adult couples class.

Attending this class and visiting with many loving and caring couples has been an inspiration over the last 40 -50 years. In fact, after being in the class for about three years, I was asked by one of the staff members to direct the Adult Department.

This department was representative of three separate classes. We would have a general gathering to discuss business, sing birthday songs, have a prayer time and then break out into individual classes.

I can tell you that there is no substitute for prayer warriors. It is my belief that walking through these years with these loving people has really built my faith in God. I have see miracles performed through prayer. No, prayer wasn't the reason for the miracles, it was the faith of the prayer warriors and God's love and blessings that made the miracles a reality.

The rewards in serving thirty years in this capacity was the sincere love of those around me and their prayers for my wife as she went through breast cancer surgery and radiation treatments. Oh yes, there was their prayers for me as I had gall bladder surgery. I will never forget these people who meant so much in my life. My wife and I still enjoy Sunday School class with all of them.

Jaycees

Another chapter of volunteerism is that of

serving as a member, board member and past President of the Russellville Jaycees.

This Jaycee chapter was not one of your normal chapters. At the time, I was selling for General Mills. My boss told me that since the Jaycees were such a viable part of the city and were so active, that any time I needed to spend with Jaycee work, to have at it.

To make a long story short, during my year as President and going to the national convention, Russellville garnered many First Place trophies with it's service to the community. This time was so self-rewarding.

One thing that I learned during this service was in listening to our parliamentarian explain why a vote was legal or not. I did understand the book on Robert's Rules of Order and try to live by them today when I am attending meetings.

Cherokee Indian Dance Team

Being of Indian descent, I have always been interested in the "Trail of Tears" and other material that was readable.

A friend of mine, Gene Burris, had two young sons. He and I were talking one day and

I suggested that we form this dance team, have a certain number of boys in it, have them make their own costumes and make it a camping program. Gene thought it was a great idea so we formed the program and opened it to boys from the ages of eleven through eighteen.

We would only have fifteen boys at a time, hold elections for Chief "Zota Moe", Medicine Man, First Brave and so on. During the fifteen years that we met, camped, danced and were in parades, we always had a list of ten to twelve boys waiting to get in. We camped religiously, year around. Rain, snow, heat, nothing stopped our camping.

Two memories that remain so vivid today were: We had a father and son overnight campout at the local camp by the name of Camp Caudle, which was sponsored by the local Kiwanis Club.

Since our dance team was the proud owners of four aluminum canoes, we would put on a campfire show for the fathers and sons. After dark, we would place one of our Indians high in a tree over the campfire. This Indian would have a cigarette lighter and a saturated ball of cotton that, when ignited, would fly straight down this wire to the fire and immediately explode. This act was identified as "fire from heaven."

The rest of the team, headed by the Chief with all his full headdress, the Medicine Man, and the First Brave would ride in the lead canoe with all of the other Indians with lighted torches, following. The tom-toms would start when the canoes would tie up below some steep rock steps that led to the fire.

At that time, the "Fire from Heaven" would ignite the fire, the Indians would enter the dance area around the fire and the dance would begin. I must tell you that Gene and I would watch very carefully as the dance team danced and the tom-tom licks were meted out to make sure they didn't get into the fire.

Normally, our Indians would depart the way they entered and you could view them from above the water, in their canoes going downstream with their torches.

My second experience is one that I will never forget. We had a new, young Indian, Scott Williams, who was there for his first outing. Gene Burris, myself and this young man were staying in a cabin. When we were ready to hit our sleeping bags that first night, Scott said, "Mr. Burris and Mr. Davis, I would like to cook you sausage and eggs for breakfast in the morning." We said that would be nice and we all turned in for the evening.

Well, in one end of the cabin there was a fireplace that was used for heating or cooking. Gene and I were awakened by the popping of the fire and there was Scott cooking his sausage. When he finished cooking the sausage and had ample grease to fry our eggs, he broke the first one, and upon turning the egg, the egg slipped over the side of the skillet and fell on the dirty rock hearth.

Scott looked back at us to see if we saw the mistake, took his spatula, moved the egg onto it and flipped it back onto the skillet. We never let on and today I know that I was the one who devoured that slipped egg, but Scott never knew that I knew.

I must tell you about Scott's packing for the first trip with the Dance Team. Scott's two brothers were members and they both had been Chiefs but neither of them had directed Scott on how to pack for a campout. Well, both of then were screaming at Scott to hurry and come on or they would be late. So, in a fit of excitement, Scott threw six eggs in the pillow case with several items, threw it over his shoulder and exclaimed, "I'm ready to go."

Well, I don't have to tell you what condition that pillow case and it's contents were in when we got to camp. Every time I see Scott, I review the packing with him and he says, "Jock, I wish you would stop telling my buddies about that time."

Our team danced in competition in Tahlequah, Oklahoma, and we paraded in every parade, including the Christmas Parade in Russellville. I can tell you that, at the conclusion of that parade, our young boys would be very cold with only loin cloths on.

During these years, many stories were told around the campfire and some of them strong enough that our young Indians did not sleep that night.

After fifteen years, Gene and I felt that we had served our time and the dance team went by the wayside. In visiting many times with Gene afterwards, we were convinced it was worth all the money, gas, tires and, yes, worry that went with heading this worthwhile program.

Today, seeing these men as grandfathers, all of them successful in their professional endeavors, we know that we helped build character and integrity in these men.

Fishers of Men

What a wonderful experience after twenty-five years of relationships to say, "This effort was worth it also." This Christian men's organization was organized some twenty-five years ago by myself and Joe Bull, a dear friend.

The organization started with four or five Christian men camping. We would leave on Wednesday morning and spend three nights on the bank of a lake, not too far away, in tents, twice a year.

Normally we would go in the middle of October and the middle of April. Most of us had boats, Coleman lanterns, Coleman cook stoves and flashlights. We would normally have our fish fry on the final night, depending on the fish that we caught, and then gather around the fire for stories. We always, even as old as we were, before hitting the sack, held hands and had a prayer time.

Our officers are elected each year with a President, Vice-President, Chaplain and Treasurer.

This was a camping group, however, and the main theme of our program is to be in care of others less fortunate. For instance, about four of our people had been informed that there was a member of our church that had become incapacitated and needed a wheelchair ramp added to his home. Within four hours, the material was furnished, carpentry work done and the ramp was ready.

There are all types of circumstances where our men help out when needed.

I suppose our membership card says it all. It states: I am a Fisher of Men, presented to (the persons name) and reads, "A Fisher of Men" Matt. 4:19 and your desire to help others in Jesus' name, and your love of nature and its elements, which were freely given by our Lord, you are accepted into this brotherhood.

On the opposite side it reads, "As a Fisher of Men I will: See to the welfare of widows and orphans. Administer to the lost. Care for the sick. Pray daily for someone. Stay mentally awake, morally straight and physically strong. Come to the aid of those in need and be helpful to this brotherhood."

I believe this says it all. These are sixteen or seventeen men who truly care for their fellow man and it is an honor and privilege for me to have served so many years with these men of God.

Friendship Community Services

What an honor and a privilege to serve many years as a Member, Board Member and past President of this service to humanity. This program evolved in 1972, however, many years before this date the program was titled "The Pope County Association for Retarded Children."

The program has grown, not only as a Pope County program but covers a large area of the state of Arkansas. Persons with disabilities are given a rightful place in their community by living in an adult-assisted environment both in living and working.

Through State and Federal grants, this organization has grown past the greatest of expectations. This program is headed up by a Board of Directors and then the leadership and full-time employment by local persons who are qualified to fill their roles.

How heartwarming it is to view the great strides that have been made through teaching and great leadership. Russellville is very fortunate to have had Mrs. Cindy Mahan as their lead over these many years.

Alumni Board of Arkansas Tech University

I am most fortunate to have been of service to my university for over sixty-four years. It has been an honor to serve as an active Board of Directors member for years, serving in the capacity of President for two different terms. Of course, Homecoming wraps the rest of the year's activities around its happenings.

Board members are elected for a three-year term and the past Presidents are active Board Members with voting rights. The year 2010 marked the year that I celebrated sixty years as a Tech Alumnus.

I am fortunate to have been voted by my peers to the Arkansas Tech Hall of Distinction. This is the highest honor bestowed upon a Tech graduate. I am honored to have held this position and all that hold this honor are invited back at Homecoming for a grand dinner and to see old friends from over the past generations. The rewards of this honor is to feel that you have served your learning institution well.

Vice President of MOAA-Military Officers Association of America

This organization is a national organization that has carried a large load in helping pass legislation that covers all of our military personnel, not only the retired officers.

Our organization meets six times annually with a dinner meeting that lasts about two hours. Speakers are invited to speak regarding updates on governmental affairs as well as others that affect our membership. Our MOAA is happy to report that we deliver several scholarships to different universities of the student's interests.

Some of our activities are: Attending and participating in local veterans affairs programs such as Veteran's Day parades, serving as President in the Salute to Freedom Committee of Pope and Yell Counties, and serving the needy in the communities.

The rewards of serving in this organization is to keep you and your family apprised of the new legislation that would affect your lifestyle, such as Tricare For Life insurance program. Also, every other month, the member and his spouse or friend get to visit with their friends and discuss points of interests.

Member of the Red Coats, Russellville Chamber of Commerce

This organization is really a prestigious job that awards a red blazer to the volunteer for the work done in relation to helping their city in any way possible. The function of the Red Coats is to be present at a new store, factory, or industry opening and help cut the tape.

The rewards of this voluntary job was to get to mingle with your friends with Red Coats. It was always a pleasure getting to tour the new facilities and rub shoulders with your friends who wore the Red Coat. It also is a pleasure to attend the annual Chamber of Commerce banquet.

Ground-breaking for the Cancer Research Center

I am so pleased to have been asked to break ground on the new Cancer Research Center in Little Rock, Arkansas.

Keep in mind that this voluntary job all happened before I knew that my wife had breast cancer. I suppose the reason I became so interested and active in this fundraiser was because I had lost my baby brother, John Edsel, to lung cancer. My wife, Melba, had lost her best friend, Janette Wilson, to pancreatic cancer. I felt this was a job I had time to do outside my normal work duties, so I accepted the opportunity.

Dr. Kent Westbrook, who became the Center's first director, called me one day and asked if I would assist he and his side kick, Betsey Blass, now deceased, in raising money in Pope County for this worthwhile cause. I readily accepted the challenge.

There were many visits in Russellville and Pope County that took place during the time that we spent together collecting funds for this center. I remember that one of our local business men, Mack Van Horn, had invited guests to his house one evening to hear Dr. Westbrook and Betsey Blass explain what this facility would do for, not only Little Rock, but the southern areas as well.

We went to work and many hours were spent driving the ways and byways getting people to dedicate their money to this worthwhile cause.

Finally, when enough funds were available

to begin the new construction, several persons were invited to the groundbreaking and Melba and I were included. I was surprised when asked if I would turn a spade of dirt with Dr. Westbrook, Dr. Suen, his assistant, and Dr. and Mrs. Alfred Crabaugh of Russellville.

Pictures were made and there was so much touching elation that it is hard to describe. Finally, I saw something to fruition that I felt we needed and thought about all of the fine friends Melba and I had lost to this dreaded disease.

At this writing, the Winthrop Paul Rockefeller Cancer Research Building is being completed, adjacent to the older Cancer Research Center. No tribute could be made to a finer man than Winthrop Paul, who himself was a huge contributor and finally lost his life to cancer.

Russellville School Board of Directors

The time I spent on the Russellville School Board was very time consuming and enlightening. I enjoyed being a part of this organization that assists the Superintendent in his planning areas. This again is a job in which the citizenry can be very opinionated in their thoughts toward administration when it comes to their children.

I would suggest to anyone who has never served on the school board, to take time to run for election, plan their running well, win the seat and then serve their area with pride and genuine interest in the kids. After all, that is what it's all about, the welfare of the children.

The rewards of this voluntary job was to see the school grow not only in brick and mortar but in academics. I was always in favor of higher salaries of our teachers and one of the main reasons is the cost of laundry and cleaning because everyone thought that each teacher should come to school dressed as if they were going to a banquet. It was fun and I enjoyed the relationships with the other board members.

Church and other community volunteering

One of the most rewarding volunteer jobs that anyone would want to do is that of doing Meals On Wheels for the shut-ins.

Our church started this program a few years back and it has meant so much to countless numbers of our elderly and shut-ins.

Those of us who are still mobile are placed on a list to deliver these meals. Usually every other month we are expected to meet at the church over a cup of hot coffee, spend about thirty minutes visiting and then it's off to see these less fortunate with containers of food, copies of the last Sunday's service, lots of goodwill in your voice and to deliver the food.

Normally, there are two to three persons that you deliver food to. These persons, being long time members of the congregation, are at an address you are familiar with or one that you know exactly where it is. You take the food and knock on the door. Slowly the person, expecting you, will appear at the door and invite you in. It could be and normally is a person who lives alone or has a care person helping watching over them. You set the food down, have a seat and the conversation begins.

Remembering how lonely my mother was, living by herself and having no one to talk to, the conversation sometimes lasts a long time, even up to an hour and covers everything about people in the church whom this person has known for years, or about the political nature of our country.

At any rate, they have someone to talk with

and are extremely happy that you are there. Anyone who has done this volunteer stint will tell you that the rewards are many and they would not miss the opportunity of helping one of these in need.

Clean-up Duties at the River Valley Christian Clinic

The local churches and other organizations take turns going over to the Christian Clinic in Dardanelle and lending a hand to clean up. This clean up happens each week, after there have been many persons, without insurance, visit the Clinic for physical or dental needs. This is a free service to them.

Prior to our departure on a bus to travel to the Clinic, we have a church furnished breakfast that morning starting at 7:00 A.M. By eight, we are all finished eating and we then load onto the church bus to drive five miles to the clinic. Upon arrival, we are given instructions on cleaning and are invited back, as Christians, to visit with and witness to the patients as they wait their turn to see the doctor.

Many of our cleaners come back over and witness to these people as they await their turn.

Through this witnessing and visiting, many of these persons have received Christ into their lives.

At any rate for the cleaning, we all don masks, rubber gloves and are off to clean. We spray an antibacterial spray on all surfaces, including chairs in the waiting room, then dry the spray with paper towels. We especially make sure that we do not miss such things such as the examination tables, lamps, foot rests, or anything else in the room including the doctor's desks.

This duty takes in the neighborhood of forty-five minutes to an hour and a half. We are then thanked by the caretaker, loaded back onto the busses and travel back to our home station with the tasks accomplished.

Everyone on the bus has a fine time visiting with the person sitting next to them. All of us have something to talk about even if is all about their aches and pains. The rewards of this program is to find out, through publications, that the donated medicine, the doctors' time and other costs, amounted to over three million dollars per year.

The greatest reward is knowing that these people would not have had medical care had it not been for the doctors, nurses, dentists, administration personnel, pharmacists, and other volunteers.

Relay for Life

All of us have been touched, either personally or in family or friends, by that awful word, cancer. Me, for instance, my baby brother died from lung cancer, my wife has survived breast cancer, my wife's best friend died from pancreatic cancer and hosts of friends who have gone on to be with the Lord who died of cancer.

May of each year, normally at the high school football field, we celebrate the lives of all these survivors by having a huge gathering of up to 5,000 persons and their families walk the track in memory of those gone on and of those who have survived. Of all the fanfare, the beautiful colors, the booths, loud speakers blaring, nothing looks so beautiful as the faces of those who have survived.

This relay is an ongoing affair that runs about twenty four hours. It kicks off with the march around the track and continues all night long, until that same time the next day. All of the monies that are received during the sales at the booths, go to the Relay For Life Fund Raiser. Our goal in 2010 was $200,000. Due to the economy being off, we raised over $180,000, which, I felt was really good.

Approximately six months before the relay, there are many meetings, seminars, reports on money raised, and just some good sense rallies. For instance, I was on a four-man steering committee that met every Monday, commencing in January and concluding in May during the relay.

Most of the money was raised through teams consisting of a captain and about fifteen fund raisers. These teams were very innovative in their sales techniques including selling T-Shirts with catchy sayings, on down to pie suppers, bake sales and yard sales. It was amazing how much money these teams brought in.

Our Co-Chairs, Hugh Dorminy and Harry Simcox, left nothing out when it came to innovations in money raising. Of course we could not leave out our full-time American Cancer Representative, Scott Dorminy. Scott was a fireball who definitely would not take no for an answer. Our computers were full every morning of calendar items that related to the relay and you had better sign off on them, or there would be twice that many the next morning.

I would say that innovation was the word to use in building this project and in keeping it going. In fact, my input to Scott was to make this a twelve-month project. I know, everyone gets tired by the time of the Relay, but with a month off, a lot of time to think, the only answer was, it was well worth it if this money saved even one life. So, if I could sum up the many rewards of this program it would be, "A fight we can all win."

The countless friends I have made through this program, the many miracles that are mentioned during this time, and most of all, hearing about those who are survivors and who weren't given a chance, has made this the most worthwhile project I've worked on. So, if you are ever asked to work in this capacity, jump at the opportunity. It is well worth it.

Salute to Freedom Committee

I could write a book about my feelings toward this program and its Director. Being a veteran of WWII and Korea and a total of 37 and one-half years of active and reserve service to my country, I felt that I really needed to give something back to those who had served during these conflicts, and others. I am sure, with OLD GLORY embedded in my heart and mind, that all of us who have served, when the red, white and blue pass, cold chills go up and down our spine.

Well, being on this important committee gives me cold chills and I will try to relay to you it's importance to me and all those like me and to our city of returning service men, school children, and city leaders.

Here goes my story. About five years ago, this man, Jim Bob Humphrey, called me one day and asked if I would serve on this committee. I told him I would think about it and after sleeping on it, I decided to go visit him.

Jim Bob, a Funeral Home owner, had embarked on the idea of his giving back to these men and women who had given so much. He had never been in service but his dad was a WWII Vet and had been through mortal hell during his service and paid the ultimate price, in the end.

Jim Bob and I sat down and discussed what the Salute to Freedom Committee did, which included the annual Veteran's Day Parade and all the programs that went with it. Several on the committee were veterans of various wars and I knew them all, plus several civic leaders, media persons, etc. who were also on the committee.

After hearing a heart rendering story about his life and how he was adopted by the Humphrey's and what he had endured a short time before within his biological makeup, I was tearful and excited to accept the challenge and told Jim Bob that I would do everything I could to help the team. We shook hands and started to work.

I have never worked with a leader the likes of Jim Bob who has the most enthusiastic, most giving heart. Monetarily and otherwise, he did twice as much as he asked of the committee members.

There is another line here that needs to be mentioned. He is supported by two of the most labor intensive ladies I have been around. Their names are Pam Peek and Anita Davis. When Anita sends you an e-mail to advise you of a Freedom meeting, your answer had better be YES, and attend the meeting or your name is mud.

I had never imagined that so much could go

into an operation such as this. For instance: Thousands of dollars must be raised, volunteers contacted for the event, all churches, bands, and schools need to be notified and the list goes on.

One of the programs that I will never forget was the one commemorating our WWII Vets. Jim Bob was set on seeing that these vets got the WELCOME HOME they deserved. During one of the early committee meetings, there were about fifteen in attendance and I asked for the floor.

Jim Bob acknowledged me and I made the following statement, "I personally thank everyone here for remembering us who came in on a train, with uniform on, duffel bag over our shoulders at midnight, with no one there to meet us and walking to our homes with all of our gear, to give our moms a hug after months of combat."

Well, after this speech of thanking all of the committee for putting this thing together, everyone there began to clap and it was very heart-warming and I wish all of the WWII Vets could have witnessed it.

From that day up on to this moment I have loved working for Jim Bob and this committee.

That Veteran's Day was a special day for all of the WWII Vets and we wanted it to be a memorable time in their lives. We asked that all the Veterans of WWII fill out a sheet explaining all of the data that was needed to cordially invite them and their spouse, or friend, to a banquet to be held at the Hughes Center in their honor.

After a feverish four or five months of raising money and planning, there was a banquet and a parade, and then a ceremony at the Depot in downtown Russellville where most of these local Vets had boarded a train long ago and gone to war. Finally, each of the WWII Veterans got the recognition that they deserved.

Of course, the banquet would not be complete without a USO background, which Jeanie McAlister did a magnificent job of duplicating.

The date came for the banquet and service men who had uniforms or parts of a uniform came with them on. There was a table to register for the Vets and their guests. There also was a huge placard there for each of them to sign, that would be saved for posterity. Jim Bob Humphrey designed all the coins for the different wars and all of them were outstanding. Each Veteran was to receive one of the coins during the banquet, presented to them by a state or local dignitary.

Renditions of WWII music was present, such as, The Chattanooga Choo-Choo, etc. The meeting was called to order by the Master of Ceremony. The Pledge of Allegiance was said and an invocation was given by one of the civic leaders.

The group then focused their attention on a huge screen on each side of the stage and a movie of President Roosevelt giving his, now famous, declaration of war. To this a standing ovation was given.

Then a picture of each veteran was shown on the screen with his rank and branch of service given. At that point the coins were distributed with a strong handshake and a "Thank You."

Then came two songs by the famous "Andrews Sisters." They even had uniforms on of the era, hairdos and hosiery to match. The songs and the singers received a huge ovation.

At the close, our Master of Ceremonies did a rendition of "Thanks for the Memories," made famous by actor Bob Hope when he would visit the troops during the war.

At the close, the colors were retrieved with everyone standing and after they were retired, Colonel Bill Eaton, one of our committee members presented a plaque to Jim Bob for his efforts to make this banquet one of the most memorable ever. Everyone gave him a standing ovation and he responded with a very emotional speech.

Pictures were made of each couple there and were sent to them following the banquet. A video is on file of the banquet and is in the files at Humphrey Funeral Home in Russellville, AR.

As the couples filed out of the Hughes Center, you could not help seeing the large illuminated USO sign that blinked a farewell to all who attended.

The next day came the three-mile long parade down West Main Street, including six bands, four fire trucks, many service organization vehicles, WWII Vets on a trailer emblazoned with red, white and blue bunting. The parade was to take one hour and conclude at the depot, where seats were available for the honorees and past veterans of all wars, their guests and anyone from the area that wished to see the happenings.

It was estimated that there were five thousand cheering, clapping, and stomping citizens who lined the downtown streets to view this spectacle. What a wonderful outing this was.

Before the start of this parade for the WWII extravaganza, the anchor of KATV Television Station in Little Rock, Scott Inman, presented Jim Bob with the Person Of The Week award that is given each week. This award showcased the importance of Jim Bob's work with the military that highlighted all of these events. The award was aired over the station in Little Rock.

Following this parade was the presentation of each Veteran, who would pass through a picture or billboard of a C-47 airplane, shake hands with dignitaries, come to the microphone state their name, rank, branch and years of service, then proceed through an honor guard made up of veterans of other wars, motorcycle groups and other dignitaries from the state and local governments.

Not only did our WWII Vets receive coins, but so did others present to commemorate this occasion.

Of course the Arkansas Tech University Band was present to play before, during and after the affair. The Arkansas Adjutant General was also present. After a forty-five minute salute to the WWII Vets, Jamie Sorrells, our Master of Ceremonies, thanked everyone for their service and those who had made this program a most successful one, bid all a goodnight and everyone was dismissed.

Well, this just set the stage for the next year and the recognition of our Korean Veterans, who too, were not welcomed home as they should have been.

Our Salute to Freedom committee began to plan, raise money and and discuss the departure of our boys from our two-county area to either Iraq or Afghanistan.

We threw out different ideas and arrived on the idea of having a huge reception for the troops and their families.

It was decided to be held at the First Baptist Church and a date was finalized.

When the date arrived, all the troops, with their families at their sides, lined up standing "At Ease." Dignitaries, and pastors from the local churches were present and we were ready to go. Jim Bob Humphrey was the Master of

Ceremonies and, as usual, did a masterful job of welcoming the troops, their families and our Committee.

He explained that we were going to pray for the troops and their families and concluding this affair, there would be snacks available on the tables against the wall and for everyone to visit with whomever they liked and they would be dismissed.

Again, Pam Peak and Anita Davis were right there working their fingers to the bone, helping the little ones and their parents share the goodies. It was a very sad affair with families and troops alike shedding tears, not knowing what their future held for them.

Within two weeks from one year, plus or minus, Jim Bob took over again and planned a homecoming for these troops, with a parade and recognition of each soldier and their families and he presented them with a challenge coin. Again, it was a great parade with all of the townspeople turning out to welcome the troops home.

One thing is for sure, as long as Jim Bob is still around, there will be recognition of our soldiers in Pope and Yell counties. Enough cannot be said about the dedication, monies yielded personally by Jim Bob, and time and effort placed in this endeavor by him. He will always be in the hearts of those who know him and admire him.

Build A Bear Program

Jim Bob had heard about a program of "Build A Bear" that included a small Teddy Bear that could talk. He had the idea that each child in a family, whose father was overseas, should receive one of these bears with the sound affect that when the child pressed the Teddy's arm a message sounded that went something like this, "Joey, be a good boy while daddy is away and remember how much I love you."

On his own, Jim Bob called the manufacturer and, without raising one cent, ordered several hundred that would be given to the children whose fathers had been called to active duty in Iraq.

The "Build a Bear" program was such a huge success that the Adjutant General of Arkansas came to Russellville and personally presented bears to a few little girls who were representative of those that would go out to all the local children.

I must tell you that today General Wofford is a real fan and will do what it takes to continue this program in the future when his troops are called to active duty.

Jim Bob has received many plaques, letters of appreciation and all types of awards in his support of our troops.

Today, and I am included, there is a national movement by Jim Bob to make the "Build a Bear" program a national program for every child of a service man, no matter what branch, to receive one of these bears. The ground work has been laid. Now for seed money to get the program off the ground, get it accepted by all branches of the military, and see that it is done.

Knowing Jim Bob and his continuous efforts toward helping our service people, IT WILL BE DONE.

Jock helping break ground at the Cancer Center in Little Rock

Left: Jock's honored friend, Mr. Jim Bob Humphrey

Below:
Soldier Bears to be given out at a homecoming for the troops

Left: *Jim Bob Humphrey presents Major General Bill Wofford a special Soldier Bear at the ceremony.*

Below: *Soldier Bear at his best*

CHAPTER 20

JOCK AND BILL CLINTON

In this era of political upheaval, we would all like to believe that the promises that are made are genuine. It is sad to think that a person who tries to live a Christian life, to be a person of integrity and believe what they are being told, could be hoodwinked into giving time, money and life, when that person you are giving it to is pulling your leg.

I am going to share with you a real life story about former Governor, and now former President, Bill Clinton and Jock Davis.

Over the years of being raised in South Arkansas, by the way, sixteen miles from Hope, Arkansas, where Bill Clinton was reared, I was taught that a Republican was a very bad name and I should never vote for anyone who was running for office under that name.

For instance, after WWII, past President Ike Eisenhower was running for President and I voted for him. I made the mistake of telling my mom that I had voted for him and you would have thought that I had voted for a convicted killer. She had me to hear that Herbert Hoover was a bad name and had brought the depression and she did not want to go into another one.

I was in my midlife cycle and knew exactly what I was doing. One day as I was having lunch, Bill Clinton called for me personally. My wife handed me the phone and said, "Bill Clinton is on the phone." Before I delve into a very sad story about my association with Bill Clinton, I will bring you up to date, prior to this phone call.

Up to this point I, as well as many other Arkansans, had become disenchanted with Clinton over several issues while he was in office, such as "Tax and Spend", which he was famous for while President.

Also we did not like the lies that had been told by him to the state populace on what he would do for the people, AND, the dress code of his young government protégé's was horrible. There were many other things that went along with these few. Well, there was a Republican by the name of Frank White who decided that he wanted to become Governor, and he threw his hat into the political arena.

Well, lo and behold he was elected Governor. In agreement with all his political platform, I agreed to work my county for him and labored hard and long on his behalf. Well, with many working hard and long for this guy, he soundly defeated Bill Clinton. I had no aspirations of getting a job in his cabinet, even though I could have gotten a state job if I had wanted it . . . but that ship seemed to have sailed.

Everyone thought that this would be the last of Bill Clinton. Not so.

Into the second half of Frank White's four years, I received this call from Bill Clinton. Bill had opened a law office in Little Rock and called to ask if I would drive to Little Rock and meet with him. The date was set and I agreed to come down for a meeting.

At the time I was a Commander of the 176th Public Affairs Detachment of the Arkansas National Guard, reporting to Major General Tom Phillips.

I asked my Executive Officer, Captain Bill Lawson if he would accompany me on my trip to see Bill Clinton, mainly as a witness.

At the time Bill Lawson worked for Blue Cross and Blue Shield and knew Bill Clinton very well.

The day arrived for me to take my trip to visit with Mr. Clinton. Bill Lawson met me at

Clinton's office. We walked into a rather quiet, subdued office without even a receptionist.

Bill and I greeted the Governor with a solid handshake, he asked us to sit down and the Governor started speaking, "Jock, I understand you have been elected as Pope County Democratic Chairman?" I responded in the affirmative.

Clinton's next words were, "Where did I go wrong in my last term as Governor?" I responded, "Governor, you lied to the people of our state. You did so many things wrong." And I named them one by one. The Governor then turned to me and asked, "If I go to the people, apologize and agree that this will never happen again, can I be reelected?" I responded, "Yes sir."

With all of this conversation and sincerity, he turned to me and said, "If I give you my word on oath that I will make it right with the people, would you serve as my campaign chairman for Pope County?" I responded by saying, "If you will do what you vow, I will serve as your chairman."

He turned toward me, shook my hand and said, "It is a deal." As I was walking toward the door with Bill Lawson, the Governor summoned me to wait a minute, which I did. He walked up to me and said, "Jock, what could I do for you if I am elected?" I said, "Governor, I do not need anything for working for you."

He insisted that I want some job in State Government and he would give it to me. He was so insistent that I said, "There would be one job that I would really like to have if you are elected, and that is to serve as your Adjutant General for the Arkansas National Guard."

As Captain Lawson was my witness, Governor Clinton stuck his finger in my chest and said, "You have got the job." Captain Lawson and I left his office both in jubilation knowing I would be the next AG and Lawson as my Exec.

I came back to Pope County, held rallies, speaking engagements, and talked my brother, Ret. Lt. Col. Edward Davis into being one of Clinton's advisors and his driver all over the state for speaking engagements. I put many thousands of miles on my personal car, paid my own expenses, I even had to have a new set of tires.

About a year through the campaigning, I held a rally at the Pope County fairgrounds with food and the works and had Clinton engaged to speak to a large crowd. About three hours before the planned speech, I received a call saying that the Governor had a conflict and asked if Hillary could fill in for him? I told them that his replacement would be fine. Hillary came, made a blockbuster speech and looking back on this affair, she would have made a much better President than he.

This campaigning went on for about two years. I could feel the tide turning for Bill and knew we had been successful. I could not wait for the day of the vote to arrive because of the pending victory. Well, sure enough, the die was cast early in the evening and the trend was set and our Pope County had gone for Clinton about four to one.

My wife and I were invited to his victory party in Little Rock. We jumped into our car and sped off to Little Rock. We were welcomed heartily by everyone at the party and a huge hug from Bill and Hillary.

There was much satisfaction in the victory and my prospects of being the next Adjutant General.

My wife and I drove back home arriving there about eleven P.M.

About eleven-thirty my phone rang and it

was the newly elected Bill Clinton on the other end of the line. I said, "Hello." The voice on the other end said, "Jock, this is Bill Clinton wanting to thank you for an overwhelming job of helping me get elected. You did a tremendous job and I will never forget it."

He then said, "You know that AG job we discussed?" I responded, "Yes." "Well, I had to give that job to Jimmy 'Red' Jones." In a great deal of remorse I said, "Governor, it is obvious that your commitment to me and the people is a lie and you have not changed a bit in your commitment," and I hung the phone up.

I met Bill Clinton on elevators and other places in Little Rock at poultry affairs, and he was always cordial and was still working for the vote. Clinton did appoint my brother, Ed, to the position of State Veterans Affairs Director. Ed held the job for about six months and resigned because of the same reason that Clinton was defeated by Frank White.

Ed believed in a strong dress code around the Capitol and Clinton's young staff members, with holes in their blue jeans and long hair and beards, did not sit well with Colonel Davis.

I always liked Bill Clinton and he was a brain and had more political savvy than most who had preceded him. There was the thing however of the beautiful ladies. Most of the stories told by the State Police during and after White Water was true. In fact, I know of one in particular that I will not address at this time.

During a lengthy illness of my brother Ed, Bill called him at Baptist Hospital in North Little Rock one afternoon and asked him how he was doing. Ed told him that he wasn't doing well at all. During the conversation, Ed asked him if the rumors were right about his run for the Presidency. Bill told him that he doubted that he would run and had promised the people of Arkansas that if they would elect him Governor for one more term that he would not run for President. You know the "rest of the story."

In watching his presidency and the way he milked his underlings dry, then cut them loose, reminded me of his treatment toward me and when the affair with Lewinsky surfaced, I was not surprised at all.

In fact, this lesson in life taught to me by Bill Clinton is one that I use in my seminars. I have built a module on two words, "Integrity" and "Commitment." I teach these seniors in land grant colleges that these two go together and you cannot have one without the other.

I had a contract with Bill Clinton and it was not based on paper. It was based on a hand shake. I still believe that my word is my bond and my word is my contract. I do thank President Bill Clinton for making me a better man.

PART 4

MY FAMILY

CHAPTER 21

MY LIFE WITH MELBA

I hope, within the next few pages, I can come near giving my lovely wife the credit she deserves for putting up with me. Just think of putting up with a spouse who travelled for fifty-odd years. She lifted my spirits when they were low, rode with me to the top when my sales were through the roof. She was there during the loss of my mother, my three loving brothers and others in my family who have gone on to be with the Lord.

Melba always wanted me to have things that, in 1948, were expensive. I was an ardent hunter, fisherman and strictly outdoors person. With the meager pay Melba earned at Plunkett-Jarrell, she first bought me a seven-horsepower outboard motor from Western Auto.

I would rent a boat at one of the local lakes, attach the small motor and I was there with the big boys. I used the motor on Lake Nimrod which, at that time, was one of the best Crappie fishing lakes in the state. Today, that motor belongs to my oldest grandson and is strictly an heirloom and is worth several thousand dollars.

Lo and behold, the next year, with Melba's budgeting, she purchased a brand new Belgian Browning, twelve-gauge shotgun, which, by the way is in the hands of my middle grandson, Josh. It too is worth several thousand dollars.

I used this gun for duck hunting. It had a thirty-inch barrel with a full choke. When the other buddies stopped firing because the ducks were out of shooting range, I would take a bead on one of the green heads and down he came. That is a whole other story about my duck hunting days with my good buddy, now deceased, Joe Bull.

Melba had so much integrity that she still possesses today. That is why she served thirty-two years travelling the state as a fraud investigator for the Employment Security Division. Melba would not sacrifice her integrity for anyone, including me. She was the only female in this position and was told bluntly, by her boss, when she was hired that she could not do the job, going up against these men. I can tell you today that if you asked her supervisor what kind job she did, he would answer, "She beat all the men in that position."

I remember well at a dinner party thrown in Melba's honor when she retired, that person after person rose to their feet paying accolades to this lady's perseverance and integrity. She still has memorabilia from that banquet that depicts her success.

I suppose the thing that rings in my ears today when I think back on these sixty-two years with Melba, she always told me that I could do anything that I set my heart and mind to. She had a tremendous way of suggesting positive assertion that would get me off my rump, stop me from feeling sorry for myself and get me moving forward.

When I think back on those days of our start in that small fiber-board trailer at Arkansas Tech University, I think, "How in the whole wide world have we accumulated what we have today?" I have a true and vital answer to that.

It is simply because of Melba's management of money. She had an ability to invest and follow her investments. She had savings that young people wouldn't even think about today. There again, she always asked my advice and I gave it to her, but someway, she would always come out on top with the right idea about an investment or savings. Melba has the exceptional mind to study a program, pick out the one she wants in place, then watch it mature.

She probably is one of the best bookkeepers I have ever met. I often tell her that I have to die first because if she did, I would just call the IRS and tell them to come get me because I know very little about the vast investments and bookkeeping that she does. In fact, our paid accountant, who does our books each year told me, "Jock, Melba has everything in such good order that we just transfer it to forms and it is ready to go." She is a phenomenal bookkeeper.

I could not have asked God for a better Christian partner than Melba. We have worked together in church as teachers in the youth department of our church. She supported me when I was Superintendent of that youth department. She supported me when I was an active deacon in my church. She supported me when I was Director of our Adult Sunday School Department and even supported me when I slipped as a sinner, not scolding me but showing me the right way that always made me feel better.

I can well remember Melba sitting down one night after supper after our twelve-year old daughter had gone to bed. She said to me these fine words that I shall never forget and wished many times that I had heeded her advice.

She said, "Jock, Jibby needs you with her now more than ever and if you do not slow down from so much volunteer work, she will be gone to college and you will
have wasted all that time."

It happened just as she said. Jibby was gone to college and I had lost those several years that she would have enjoyed and I most assuredly would have enjoyed. What a lesson in life she tried to teach me and I did not listen.

Since that time, I have tried to listen more closely to my wonderful wife. I, like most Christians, keep waiting for some word from our Lord, but, with that human element, we do not listen. Oh, how I wish that I had listened to my dear wife more in the past. Life would have been more tolerable.

Melba has caught the eyes of her little, great-grand daughters, Hannah and Caitlin. When they are around and you hear them call out her name, "Memaw", you know she is getting into their hearts. Why shouldn't she? Their dad has "Memaw" in his heart, as has all three of these grown military men.

I do want to say to Cain, Josh and Zach, "Men don't ever forget the teachings of integrity that your Grandmother taught you as you grew up. How she has prayed and worried over you when you were on your missions, flying an Apache Helicopter from Kuwait during the invasion of Iraq. She would follow your exploits through television at 3:00 in the morning with tears streaming down her face in fear for your lives. From the day you were born, up and until this day and forward, she will be very concerned over you and your family's lives."

This dissertation would not be complete without talking about what a wonderful cook and homemaker Melba is. She has always planned her meals with health in mind. Purchasing products that carry the label as being healthful. I have never put a morsel in my mouth that she prepared that wasn't tasty and good for you and your longevity. Of course, donuts are a downfall for me and when I am gorging myself with these tasty morsels, I can hear her in my subconscious saying, "Go ahead and kill yourself."

If you ask my grandsons how the food was she sent them in Iraq and Afghanistan, their response would be "Jock, it was all good, but, the oat bran raisin cookies were the best. She made them from scratch.

Her coconut pie could win blue ribbons in every fair in the United States. My grandsons will attest to that.

I failed to mention the fact that Melba doesn't particularly like golf, but, when I mention going to play golf at my course, which is John Daly's, she will say "Do well today." In fact, if there is a day that can be tolerated with just enough heat to keep the balls warm, she will say, "Sure would be a nice day for golf."

Oh yes, with relation to my golf game, she often says, "I can always tell when Jock has a good day at the course. He will come in smiling, and cracking jokes, etc. But when he comes in quiet and has little say at the dinner table, I know then that things did not go well."

Really, this book, "Brothers Four", could be written on the "Merits of Melba." There is not enough paper or thoughts for me to describe this beautiful lady, inside and out. How, in this sixty-two year span she has put up with late hours, cancelling trips, being gone to Jaycee meetings, playing golf, church work, volunteer for this and that, miss a trip to a high school football game to take the cheer leaders, and the list goes on.

I suppose, through all this life of Melba's, none of her life has been for herself. She is probably the most unselfish, family-caring, God-loving lady I have ever known.

I truly believe if I have been successful in life, I owe 100% of it to Melba Jean Thompson Davis. Without her guidance, commitment, integrity and most of all love, I could have done nothing.

I thank Almighty God for sending her to Arkansas Tech University. I know in my own heart that she was the one who was destined to marry and care for Jock Davis.

Jibby Davis Baker

Oh yes, there is Jibby Davis Baker, my only child and she is so loving. What a personality. If you ever meet Jibby you will never, ever, forget her. Jibby knows the meaning of sacrifice and patriotism with her husband and three sons serving in harms way. With constant prayer and reverence to God, she rose above adversity and is in her 26th year of teaching in the Georgia schools and soon plans to retire.

I have tried to pass accolades on to my family who have given the ultimate sacrifice in serving their country: My son-in-law, retired Lt. Colonel Phil Baker, now a director of one of the best ROTC programs in a high school in Georgia, Major Phillip Baker, Aviation, soon to be Lt. Colonel, now serving in the Pentagon, Major Joshua Baker, service at the Red Stone Arsenal in Huntsville, AL, and destined to be a Lt. Colonel soon and Captain Zachary Baker, on his second tour in Iraq with the 101st Airborne, whose next move is to Major. All of these have distinguished themselves in battle far above what I witnessed in WWII. I know that you have seen just how proud I am of all of my family.

Left: Beautiful daughter, "Jibby" Davis

CHAPTER 22

MY GRANDSONS

I would be remiss if I did not mention the wonderful times that I enjoyed with my two oldest grandsons while their dad was in Korea. Our youngest grandson, Zach, had not been born then.

I probably spent more time with Cain, the oldest, because he was older and loved hiking and the outdoors. Josh was only about four or five years old and wanted to be near his mom.

Those afternoons visiting the bluff area on the Arkansas River after church were probably the most memorable and loving days that a grandpa could spend with his grandson.

Nature holds so many intriguing adventures and words cannot explain them, but I did my best to parlay nature's meaning by starting with the name "God". From that name, there were many questions asked and there were many answers that seemed to satisfy and intrigue Cain.

Often, Cain would ask questions that would interest me and test my knowledge, but some way or some how, I got the job done. The time that was spent on these beautiful, Sunday afternoons lasted about four or five hours, making sure he was home in time to go to evening services at the First Baptist Church.

I cannot forget the memories of our outings together. Josh, as a little brother, fishing beside his brother Cain, and with Cain catching one after the other, Josh would say, "Move over Cain and let me fish there." Of course, being a caring and loving brother, Cain would move over and let Josh have his place.

I suppose the most moving of all I could write was when Cain, two or three years later, while they were stationed at another Fort, sent me a three ring notebook that he had made at school. In this book, there was page after page of things that happened in his young life, many of them that contained pictures of he and I. After thumbing through the book, I noticed the last two pages included a large picture of he and I when we made our trip, just the two of us, to the slopes in Colorado.

In looking at the picture, it brought back memories of this ski trip: our kneeling by our bed at night and having a prayer time, thanking God for our safety and the good times we were enjoying. When I finished surveying the picture, there was a full page handwritten note. (I wish you could read it in its original form. It is a special note that he included in his notebook that was turned in for a grade at school.)

I must tell you that my eyes swelled to tears so, that I had to stop reading half-way through his presentation. I will never forget how proud I was that this little boy, my grandson, had this deep inner feeling in his heart for his grandfather.

I love all three of these grandsons equally, but to see and hear that I had done the right thing in Cain's life, made this association extra special.

While feeling the pride, patriotism, and love of these three young men, memories continue to flood my brain of their growing up under the influence of their dad, the loving care of their mom and serving around the globe.

Sacrifice is something we cannot mention enough, considering the sacrifices of our young men to protect their country and their countrymen.

As was said by an intellectual, "Memories of days are forgotten, but moments of memories last forever." This is so true.

I think about the oldest, Cain, now a father of

two beautiful little girls, Hannah and Caitlin. Melba and I love them up every time we have the opportunity. Cain's wife, Courtney, also graduated from Auburn and is a wonderful mom and wife, supporting the other wives in the Battalion while the husbands are away.

I know that these young men are destined to become very decorated soldiers with high ranking.

Cain is destined to become a Battalion Commander at the young age of 37, carrying the rank of Lt. Colonel. There is no doubt in my mind that he will achieve the rank of Colonel and maybe General, before his retirement.

Josh, with a degree from Auburn in Aviation Management, is now 34 years of age and just attained the rank of Major. He is destined to become at least a Colonel and probably destined to head a huge company that produces for the military. Josh is married to Haley, who graduated from Western Kentucky University. Haley is a reporter for a Television Station in Huntsville, Alabama. They have no children.

Zach, a graduate of University of Alabama, should attain the rank of Lt. Colonel or higher as an Infantry foot soldier. Zach, now a Captain, is stationed with the101st Airborne at Ft.

Campbell and he is married to Ana, who also graduated from the University of Alabama.

I failed to mention that Cain and Zach both attended Ranger School. Both boys graduated with high honors with Cain receiving the William O. Darby Award.

I know that my expectations are high for these young men and should be. They are all born again Christians and live lives that are conducive to their commitment to Christ.

I could write a book about these treasures of memories with my grandsons. I only wish Zach had been older and I could have spent the same amount of time and had fun with him as well, but due to his being overseas so long with his parents, it was impossible.

Being retired military, I had the opportunity to make over sixteen hops overseas to visit these boys and their parents.

I would catch a flight on a KC-135 refueler out of Little Rock Air Force Base and fly into Ramstein, Germany, and the two boys and their dad would pick me up there. The cost was $20 round trip and $3 for a sack lunch to carry aboard and have a snack on the flight.

You retired guys should take one of these hops with your wives. It is fascinating.

I am happy to report that all three of these young men have committed their life to Christ. I am sure that with the invasion of Iraq and duty there after, that the thought of Christ has been on their minds constantly.

All of them were in ROTC, using the military program to supply their grants, even though they have paid back the Government grants that were afforded them. They were all excellent students, graduating high in their areas of study.

My, how I remember the times they spent with me, especially the two older ones, hiking, camping, snow skiing, fishing, swimming and all types of activities. I did my best to teach them the facts of life in a Christian manner and when they visited me, we always attended Church.

I remember while their father was in Korea, my daughter and the two older boys lived near Melba and I, and after church on Sunday, we would either eat out or eat at our house. These were memorable and loving times. Of course I spoiled them and would do it over again, given the opportunity.

They have always been good young men and are setting a good example for their children.

Who knows what the future will bring to these young people as they continue to grow in many ways. I will continue to counsel, when asked, and do whatever is necessary to help release the load of life on all of them.

Yes, these young men have made me proud and I have a flag and a yellow ribbon on a tree commemorating their service in combat. When Old Glory waves in the breeze or when it passes by during a Veteran's Day parade, cold chills pass through my body.

I know that the blood shed, even today, from our service men and their patriotism will never be forgotten.

My how I remember those memories of years past and the glorious time these young grandsons and I shared and loved so much.

Josh and Cain, in high school, admiring their catch

Above: Capt. Josh Baker and his granddad, "Jock," home from Iraq
Below: Capt. Josh Baker, arriving home in the early hours from Iraq

Above: L to R, Wife Melba, Capt. Josh, Haley (Josh's wife) and Jock
Below: Josh stands in front of his Apache, "ready to go"

Above Lt: Capt. Josh standing in the Green Zone after the takeover of Iraq

Above Rt: Ltc. Cain Baker
Below: L to R, Lt. Josh, 2nd Lt. Zach, Capt. Cain and Jock

Left: *Josh, Jock, Cain, and Zach, big buddies*

Below: *Zach's mom and Lt. Baker at Ranger graduation at Ft. Benning*

Above: L to R, Lt. Zach Baker, Ltc. Ret. Phil Baker, General Petraeus, Zach's mom, at Zach's Ranger graduation
Below: 2nd Lt. Zach Baker and brother Cain at Zach's commissioning

Above: Haley and Major Josh at Taylor Marie's christianing
Below: Zach, Jonah Lawrence, and Ana before Zach's departure for Iraq

Above: Cait, Courtney, Hannah, and Cain at Hilton Head
Below: (Left) Ltc. Cain Baker, (Right) Major Josh Baker

Above: Captain Zach Baker
Below: Ltc. Cain Baker and his grandpa, Jock, at the Tomb of the Unknown Soldier in Arlington

Captain Zachary Baker and his wife Ana at their wedding

CHAPTER 23

THE REAL ED DAVIS

Being one of the brothers of Ed Davis was a delight and I enjoy writing about him. I am sure that there are many instances that will be rekindled in my mind by the time this book is published.

It is my pleasure for the readership to understand why there was so much sincere love between the four of us.

THE SAGA OF A LOVING SON

Ed loved dogs. My first recollection of Ed's encounter with a dog was on Mother's Day.

Evidently, on Ed's paper route, which he walked every day, there was a house that had a female that had given birth to several puppies. To Ed's delight, he would stop by, in the garage where the dogs stayed and love up the puppies.

One particular Mother's Day, on coming home from the route, he hollered, "Hey Mom." Mom answered him in a loving way as mothers do and asked him what he wanted. He said, "Mom, I have you a Mother's Day present." He handed her this little, spotted six-week-old puppy. Mom, with a firm expression on her face said, "Oh Ed, that was so sweet of you to remember me." Ed then walked away pleased that he had gotten "Mom" something for Mother's Day that did not cost a cent.

THE SAGA OF THE RABID DOG

Again, Ed's love of dogs, especially cur dogs, was as pure a love as a 12 or 13-year-old youngster could want.

Again, on his paper route, a little cur dog either followed him home or someone gave him to Ed. He loved playing with his dog, going to the creek, swimming and throwing sticks for this dog to retrieve. Well, during this period of time there were no rabies vaccinations for dogs.

As luck would have it, this little dog began to bark, run in circles and froth from the mouth. Almost every time this was a pure indication of the dog being mad.

Ed kept this hidden as long as possible from Dad. Dad came in early one afternoon and this dog went into one of his fits. Dad came into the house, summoned Ed to his side and said,

"Ed, I am sorry to tell you that you must put your dog away tomorrow." Tears swelled in Ed's eyes and he left the room. It was obvious that his best friend, this little cur dog, was going to die.

Early the next morning, Ed loaded his 20-gauge shotgun with ammo, placed a rope around his dog's neck and started off toward the pasture without saying a word to anyone.

After this awful deed was accomplished, Ed never seemed to be the same until manhood. He would sit around the house, read a book, not look up and would answer only if talked to.

His best friend had left him for good. As far as I know, Ed never owned another dog.

THE SAGA OF THE BANK WINDOWS

As I mentioned, we all walked to deliver our newspapers.

We first delivered our papers to the residential sections of town and then delivered to the stores downtown.

You had to know Ed. Ed was very quiet, loved to sleep and was a sleepy head for an hour or two after getting up about 5:00 A.M. to deliver papers.

The three of us had delivered our papers in residence and were going door to door downtown.

The only bank in town was on a corner and, during the summer time, they left some swing-out windows open to air the bank. These windows opened up to reach about two or three feet. Roy, my oldest brother was always in the lead and Ed was next with me, the younger, bringing up the rear.

As we approached the windows, Roy swung way out to miss the windows. Unbelievably, Ed's head hit each window. I heard him crying and I said, "Ed, why are you crying?" and he answered and said, "I bumped my head on those windows and it hurts." I know this happened several times after that, but Ed was so sleepy he just couldn't wake up.

These are just a few of the instances that I remember of my loved and departed brother Ed. I just had to share them with you.

Just think, after all this, Ed was a tremendous mathematician, had tremendous grades in high school and without a degree was one of the most highly decorated pilots during WWII. I am so proud of Ed, as well as John and Roy.

LTC. EDWARD W. DAVIS

"A WWII HERO"

At least that is what we three brothers thought of Ed Davis and his heroics while flying his B-26 Marauder Bomber over Germany and making strikes with his crew in skip bombing that was very necessary to help end this mighty war.

In reflecting back on our days as young boys, with no money, very little to eat, scarce clothing and shoes, there was so much love between us that we never thought of fighting each other, in fact we always thought of supporting each other in any way possible to offset some of the uncertainties that existed during the "Great Depression."

Ed had probably the most serious personality of the four boys. I will not use the word "lazy" to describe Ed. I suppose he just wanted to be left alone to read one of his "Big Little Books" or comic books, while reclining on the old couch on a clear, sunny day or busy himself studying his lesson for the next day of class or working on a new model airplane that he saved his nickels and dimes to buy.

I can remember well, at the age of thirteen or fourteen, that Ed would quietly drift off to his paste-board drafting board, pull out a little box of parts and start assembling his British Spad, Bi-wing model, while we other boys were out playing football, shinney, pitching washers or washing Dad's A-Model Coupe.

The models cost between twenty-five and fifty cents and were a maze of balsa wood and glue, plus the flimsy paper that was used to cover the fuselage and wings when the proper engineering was done to frame the plane. Ed also used some type of liquid to brush on the paper to make it tighten and shine.

Of course, at that time there were no gas engines to assemble, only a rubber band that ran from the propeller to the rear of the plane. When wanting to fly it you would wind the prop in a certain direction and when the proper pressure was applied, you gently tossed the aircraft into the sky and in a short time the prop would stop and the little plane would glide to a safe landing. I have seen Ed, many times, go into the pasture by our house and over and over he would toss his aircraft into the air and enjoy seeing it come to a gentle landing.

To know Ed was to love him. If there ever was a person who was destined to become a pilot, Ed was that person. His love of aeronautics, his love of math and his love of being able to fly some day was only exceeded by his love of his God, family and country.

During the thirties and forties, athletes were not the size that they are today. Ed, out of the four of us, carried a larger size. He and Roy, my oldest brother, were quite a bit taller than John and I. We all played football for Prescott High School, but none succeeded as well as Ed. He wasn't fast but, as a tackle, he could lay a hit on a running back that could be heard at the top of the stadium. While being a boy of few words, Ed, when given a task, did his job, did it right and excelled in everything.

Upon graduation from high school, Ed gained a scholarship to the University of Arkansas and in August, Mom packed his gear in a paste board box and he rode a bus to Fayetteville to find his fortune in college football, as a tackle for the Razorbacks.

Unfortunately, before the season started, while practicing, an injured knee caused him to withdraw from the team and since there was no scholarship now and no money to go to school, a dejected Ed came home with his head hanging low.

During this time, in the late thirties and early forties, the depression was in full swing and no jobs were to be found. At that time, young people were taken into the CCC. This stood for Civilian Conservation Corps. The pay was meager but at least his widowed mother did not have to plan for another mouth to feed. Ed was off to Hollis, Arkansas, a few miles from Hot Springs. Today, the CCC buildings still stand in Hollis and the government has made it into a park that lists where the barracks stood as well as the mess halls, latrines and other buildings.

Before the attack on Pearl Harbor, Ed had heard of an opportunity to join the Army Medical Corps and be stationed at the Army/Navy Hospital in Hot Springs, Arkansas, as a corpsman.

Not long after entering the Army, there was a pretty little registered nurse that was from Kansas City who had been introduced to Ed. Not long after this courtship, Ed and Barbara were married.

There was a directive that came out, after the bombing of Pearl Harbor, that America was needing pilots and you could take an entrance exam and if you passed it, you could become a pilot. This was right down Ed's line. He requested the exam, passed it with flying colors and was off to flight school in Texas.

You must remember that math played a huge part in flying, therefore, Ed was made for the exam and his dreams were becoming a reality.

At that time the AT-6 Primary Trainer was the craft needed to teach young pilots to fly. Part of the flight training was physical aptitude. I remember seeing a picture of Ed after three months of training and a lot of physical activity, Ed had lost many pounds and was hard to recognize.

Upon receiving his commission as a 2nd Lt. and his silver wings, Ed was directed overseas and was stationed somewhere at a base in England.

Our family knew that Ed would be flying the B-26 Marauder Bomber that carried two engines and was very adept at carrying a huge load of bombs and firepower. When this bomber first came out, it was termed "The Flying Coffin" because so many of them crashed and many lives were lost. Finally, after working with the plane, the manufacturer came out with different versions and the B-26 became a real factor in the war.

The first time that Ed and I visited after his return from overseas, he said little but he did share with me some of the strife he endured.

He mentioned that he and his crew had had a tough run over Germany and somewhere along the bomb drops, his plane picked up a mass of Ack-Ack from anti-aircraft fire from the ground and he knew the hits that were made on his plane were from shrapnel. He and his crew made it back safely to their base and when he started to land he noticed that there was no response from his steering. There was only one thing to do and that was to try to land the plane by using the trim tabs, which was a small crank that was located above the pilot's head. He managed to get the plane on the ground in the dark. The next morning, he and his crew assessed the damage and you could see light through the fuselage.

Ed did talk a lot about when they met in the ready room preparing for a bombing run. He said you could view the seriousness on the faces of the pilots and their crews with the question on all of their minds, "Will this be the last run for me?" Evidently, the ones who never returned somehow knew that this was their last run.

Ed also shared with me the dangers of "skip bombing." His squadron was making a run on dikes in Holland. His plane and crew would come in really low over the dikes, after dark, release their bombs and the fireworks display was unreal. He said that at times it seemed that wood the size of cross ties appeared as though they were coming into his cockpit.

Now, those of us who never experienced combat flight will never know the "heroism" that existed in the hearts of these pilots and the price they paid to fight for the freedom that we all enjoy today.

My mother shared with me, through a letter, while I was in New Guinea, that Ed was very worried about his little brother, Jock. On the other hand, I was very worried about all my brothers and my mom. With the communications as they were back then, the only thing you had was occasionally an Army Times that told you about the war in Europe. We pretty well knew what was going on in the Pacific.

Ed shared with me a happening that took him to his knees after he returned home. He and

Barbara were stationed at Barksdale Field in Shreveport, LA. One day, as they were walking down the street, he recognized one of his flying buddies coming toward him with only one leg. Ed said, "With tears streaming, I grabbed my buddy and said, 'The last time I saw you, you were in a flat spin, smoke billowing and then the crash of your plane. I never saw a chute or anyone bail out, what happened?' The other pilot said, 'Ed, I finally bailed out, kicked my way out from the under the craft, opened my chute and was captured by Germans. My leg had to be amputated because of the injury.'" How is this for a war story?

Ed never mentioned his commendations. I know for sure there were Distinguished Flying Crosses with Oak Leaf Clusters, Good Conduct Medals, Air Medals with Oak Leaf Clusters and many more that probably make him one of the most decorated pilots in WWII.

I will never forget how handsome he was in full dress uniform. Dressed out with his dark-green, OD, blouse and his pinks, with trousers, adorned with his ribbons that represented years of sacrifice for he and his family, he looked to be one of the most patriotic military men I have been around.

Even after Ed retired from the Air Force, he spent time building model airplanes with gas engines. It was nothing for him to build one that had a five-foot wingspan. He enjoyed belonging to groups who flew models and I imagine most of them were retired military pilots.

I suppose one of the most moving times in my life with Ed was about two or three years before he passed away. At that time, Ed was Executive Secretary for the Arkansas Telephone Association. As usual, he did a marvellous job using that smile and hard work, going to Washington and lobbying for his association.

One day I called him and said, Ed, I'm going to be in Little Rock tomorrow and I would like to have lunch with you at the Base, at the Officer's Club. He agreed and the next day Ed was there waiting for me. He gave me a big hug, which he always did and we sat down to break bread.

We discussed old times. We had just lost our youngest brother and we talked about him and his family. We talked about my family.

Finally, when we were finished and almost ready to leave, I said to him, "Ed, I would like to ask you a personal question and if you don't feel like answering, then just don't answer." He said, "What's the question, Jock?" I said, "Do you know the Lord as your personal Savior?" His answer was, "Little brother, I settled that thing a long time ago overseas." We departed and both of us were very relieved and happy.

As I wrote earlier, I had the honor of standing at the WWII Memorial in Washington, DC, and I had the humble pleasure of observing Ed's B-26 Bomber in the Smithsonian Institution. As I looked at this plane, I thought of my brother, my real hero. A man who gave his all for his country. A man who appreciated the freedoms that America has to offer. The freedom which he protected in order that his offspring could live safely in a society that other countries would like to call home.

The only word that comes to mind that typifies all four of us brothers is LOVE.

Jock stands proudly beside his brother's B-26, "Flak Bait," in the Smithsonian in Washington, D.C.

CHAPTER 24

WORLD WAR II MEMORIAL

I was one of the first persons donating to the fund to build the WWII Memorial in Washington D.C. I am sure every veteran of that war would enjoy walking the mall of that sacred place and thinking back on their service.

I did have a friend, T-Sgt. David Murdoch of my city, who was invited by Honor Flights to received a free flight, with about 150 other veterans, to fly to Washington, spend the day and return before evening. He was simply blown away with the courtesies extended to himself and the many others who made the flight. Their ages ranged between eighty-six and ninety-eight years of age.

Well, Thanksgiving of 2010, my wife, Melba, and I, were invited by our oldest grandson, Major Cain Baker, now stationed at the Pentagon, to fly up, spend four days with he and his family and tour the memorials. Of course this was very inviting since we would be with our lovely grand-daughter in-law and our beautiful two great-granddaughters, Hannah and Caitlin.

We were greeted by Major Baker at the Reagan Airport and drove to Alexandria, Virginia, to his home. Of course, I had been to Washington before and had the opportunity to view my brother's WWII B-26 which is housed in the Smithsonian Institute but, at that time, there was no WWII Memorial to view.

While passing all the historical points in Washington on our route to his home, it was very interesting to view George Washington's home and several other points of interest that simply took your breath away.

Of course, the Potomac ran the complete length of the drive and is breathtaking also.

We settled into our "home" for four days and the next morning we dressed for the cool air and boarded Major Baker's car for the drive to our first stop, the WWII Memorial.

What a beautiful structure. So expansive and breathtaking. Fountain areas are everywhere and granite adorns the entire structure. Each state is engraved around the Memorial.

I began to think back on all my buddies I had shared sadness and and gladness with while in New Guinea, Australia and the Philippines. I wondered just how many of them were still alive and how many of them had the opportunity to view this structure.

As my wife and I stood arm in arm together, three beautiful young ladies from California approached us and asked, "Sir, did you serve in WWII?" I told them where I was from and "yes" I had indeed served in WWII in combat with two battle stars and had also, after being recalled, served during the Korean War.

One of the young ladies mentioned that their grandfather had served in WWII. They asked me if I would share experiences I had in combat in New Guinea and the Philippines. I accommodated them with several stories, and I could tell that they were keenly interested in me and my service.

I was proud to tell them that not only I had served out of my family but also my three brothers, two in the Air Corps, one in the Marines and of course, me, who served in the army.

They even asked how I felt about patriotism, and I gladly supplied them with all the feelings that were in my eighteen-year-old heart as I passed from beneath the Golden Gate Bridge, heading for the South Pacific. I also shared that when I view Old Glory at any type of gathering, cold chills run up and down my legs.

I must say that I was really humbled by the people who continued to walk up to me and say, "Thank you so very much for your service."

Our next move was to walk to the Korean Memorial. I probably was most impressed by the number of Asians who were present at this Monument.

My grandson was taking pictures, a few of which I shared in this book, of my wife and I as we travelled from Memorial to Memorial.

While Major Baker was taking my picture, I looked and noticed at least 100 people whom I thought were of Korean descent, standing, watching him take pictures of me with the figures in the background. I asked him to ask one of the Koreans to have their picture made with an old Korean War Vet.

Before he could stop the swell, there must have been at least fifty men and women standing single file, waiting to have their picture made with me. Of course, this was a wonderful opportunity for them to get pictures of themselves along with me at this great memorial. I suppose my cap said it all: Army Retired.

We made the long walk from the Korean Memorial to the Lincoln Memorial. After seeing pictures of Mr. Lincoln sitting there in the lights with people admiring, we finally got to personally stand there and view the sights and sounds of the Lincoln Memorial.

To see pictures of days gone by and the rough lives people lived during civil strife and hear remarks said about the memorial was heart-warming.

Through our travels of that day I will never forget being amazed at the numbers of people who were from foreign countries. I would say the Americans were outnumbered by six or seven to one.

Cameras were the order of the day and I am sure that my wife and I appeared in pictures around the globe.

I suppose the most sobering walk was the one from the parking lot that led to the Arlington Cemetery and the Tomb of the Unknown Soldier.

As we walked by the thousands of graves that are so wonderfully marked, I thought of my comrades, of whom I know many have passed away, who made the ultimate sacrifice for their country.

As the cool breeze rushed through our body and we stood there, viewing the fall colors of the maples, all types of thoughts ran through my mind as well as a few swelling tears in my eyes.

I suppose the highlight of all the sights that were seen that one day was the Tomb Of The Unknown Soldier. While viewing the strict discipline of that soldier who marched to the end of the line, snapped his heels together and did an "About Face", I thought about this unknown one who had so gallantly serving his country. Of all the sightings that day, during the viewing of the "Tomb", there was not a whisper by anyone and everyone stood in silence at attention while this ongoing tribute was being given to this one who gave so much.

Well, the tour was not over. We drove once more to the Smithsonian Institution and went to the Aviation section to observe Ed's B-26 Bomber.

It felt like we must have walked ten miles that day, but I am sure it wasn't that far. We finally arrived at the building where Ed's Bomber Fuselage lay on the floor, showing the cockpit, the co-pilot's seat and the navigator's seat. It was as if I could see my brother as a

Command Pilot flying his plane in for a bomb run.

I remember Ed's wife, Barbara, sharing with me the only time that Ed had an opportunity to view his plane there, he stood with tears running down his cheeks in thought of memories of those years.

One area I would have liked to have seen, and we did drive by it, was the World War I Memorial that was under re-construction. I do hope that I might have the opportunity to see this one day because my dad never had that opportunity, even though he was a wounded veteran of World War I.

As I lay awake that night reviewing the sights of the day, I could not help but think of what had transpired since 1945. When you view the advances in technology that has grown by leaps and bounds with regards to our military, in the air, on the ground, and on the sea, it even makes you more proud to be a veteran of "long ago."

Weaponry is one thing you must have to fight a war and win. I believe we have the best minds in the world when it comes to technology. It will even get better as time goes on.

Well, I finally had the opportunity to visit the places that I wondered if I ever would get to visit. I was overwhelmed by what I saw, by the respect of the men and women who I met on the grounds and most of all, the respect that our statesmen have for those of us who have served.

I do wish someday that there would be a memorial for all of those who served in support of those who fought. For instance, "Rosie the Riveter", ammunition makers, ship builders, vehicle builders, and every aspect of support that these people gave, which helped us do our job. Maybe someone, someday, will come up with idea, present it to the congress and get a memorial underway.

After returning home, I have spent many hours looking at pictures, rehashing memories of our walk and spending time with my lovely granddaughter-in-law and my great-granddaughters.

I hope Honor Flights speeds up their flights and sees to it, before they are all gone, that every World War II Veteran has an opportunity to view this magnificent structure. I know they will be blown away just as I was. It was a most memorable and loving trip. Many thanks to my grandson, Major Cain Baker, and his family, who made this trip possible.

Above: Proudly laid to rest in Arlington Cemetery Left: Jock stands proudly at the Korean War Memorial

with a South Korean National

<u>Above:</u> *Jock and Melba at the WWII Memorial in Washington, D.C.*
<u>Below:</u> *Jock at the Lincoln Memorial*

CHAPTER 25

MY REFLECTIONS ON DR. MORGAN

For over forty years I have been visiting Mississippi State University. My first visits before Dr. Morgan became Department Head were involved with recruiting for the Poultry Industry. I must say that there were some recruits who are still involved in poultry today that are very successful in the industry.

For the remaining twenty seven or so years I have been involved in teaching a seminar that involves seniors at MSU that are in Poultry Science. Dr. Morgan has always been an instrument in getting the best for his students in academia.

Dr. Morgan is absolutely the best friend I have ever had. He was always there for me when I needed advice, direction or anything else that he could do for me or my family. Our long visits while on the course involved the best of humor and the poorest game of golf. I always had a blast playing golf with him although he usually had to have a dollar to hang on his wall to chastise me.

I never found Wallace a person to lie, always

carried with him the utmost in integrity and love for his fellow man that could not be exceeded by anyone. Although, his mishaps are many, he still never complains about them but always lifts someone else up, who is less fortunate.

In our many conversations the word LOVE Is used extensively and when we meet he always gives me that big bear hug, which means, "Man, I love you." Wallace always puts his life in the proper perspective, God, family and work. He knows where to place the emphasis and does it well.

Wallace, even though I am not there in person, my spirit is with you and always will be, and that includes your lovely wife and children.

May God bless you in many-many years of healthy retirement and I look forward to seeing you on the golf course soon.

Love You, Jock and Melba Davis

CHAPTER 26

A BIG CREDIT TO DR. TOM WALKER

There are not enough words to credit Dr. Tom Walker with reference to my spiritual growth since I have known him. Even though Dr. Tom has been on the staff of First Baptist and then eventually the Associate Pastor, he has really made the largest impact on my life the last twelve to fifteen years.

During this period of time, those who desired Wednesday night prayer meeting services, have moved from the sanctuary to one of the Sunday School rooms for services. It is sad to say that out of the approximately 1700 members of this church, only 30-35 faithful meet each Wednesday evening. Also, it is disheartening to see only the faithful membership, a few deacons and our pastor has been there these years by the numbers you can count on your fingers.

All of us, who consider ourselves Christians, are looking for spiritual food by someone who has the knowledge to pass it on to us.

I grew up being sprinkled in a Central Presbyterian Church and then after marriage, I joined the Southern Baptists and have been associated ever since. From the tender age of seventeen, getting ready to go overseas during WWII, I gave my heart to Christ. Since that time, I have never found anyone who could convey the Word as clearly and as eloquently as Dr. Tom.

This man can reel off passages from the tip of his tongue and never miss a word. He has the uncanny knack of keeping your attention. His constant, "Now listen to me." Or "You look like you doubt me," is consistently heard during his sermons. There is no doubt in my mind or in the minds of others the "Walk" of this individual.

Just a side-bar to his teachings on Wednesday evenings: Dr. Tom continually visits the hospitals, not only in Russellville but all over Little Rock. If there is a need of counseling, he is always ready and willing to serve. On Sunday, before Veterans Day, he always has a service planned to honor the veterans and those who have fallen. His dad, now deceased, was a WWII Veteran, and he lets everyone know it.

Dr. Tom, partially retired with his main focus and part-time employment with the church, is working with the elderly. Most of his time is taken with this group in monthly luncheons, conducting funerals for those who pass and preaching on Wednesday evenings.

Everyone who attends a church, no matter what denomination, are fully aware of who Dr. Tom Walker is.

I am convinced of one thing. Dr. Tom has a special place awaiting him when he gets to Heaven.

To Dr. Tom, I would like to say: You have been such a blessing to my wife and me. The many hours that you have spent preparing and studying the Word is reflected in your WALK and your TALK. What a blessing it has been these past twenty or thirty years just to be called your friend. May God bless and keep you as you continue to proclaim His Word.

CONCLUSION

I have spent many hours at the computer mulling over the words, memories and thoughts that I could convey to you, the reader.

I have always felt and still do to this day that when you have done all you can do, strap on your gear and move forward, because there is still fifteen percent more that can be done in that day.

If you do not remember anything I have written, I wish you would remember one thing, "To expect more is to get more."

In writing this book I have tried my very best to relay to my readership how wonderful family life was during the depression years.

Memories are so vivid of the sincere love and affection that we four boys had for one another. Just the thought of my brothers being in harm's way during the war brought chills up and down my spine.

While trying to sleep in the jungles of New Guinea, thoughts at night would pass through my head about my brother on his bomb runs over Germany, if he was shot down, wounded, etc., or worrying about how my widowed mom was doing coping with two of us overseas and wondering of her thoughts while she watched the mailman carefully as he approached the front porch, with possibly bad news. I worried if she was being cared for with food, clothing and the essentials. As a boy of eighteen years, I was much older in thought and deed than that of a young man of today.

However, all of us warriors had a job to do, no matter where it led us.

My brothers, all patriotic warriors, did the job they were given without a whimper. They came home winners, accepted their place in life, continued their journey into the unknown and accepted those things that were meted out to them.

Deep down in my heart, I know they are in heaven enjoying the wonders of beauty that we have all been taught about in the Word.

I, as a military retiree, have been very disappointed in the manner in which our country has dealt with our fighting men. Even though the morality of our country has dropped to a new low, I still believe in America and its foundation, our Constitution, and our government.

I believe God is giving the USA another chance to make amends and if we do not listen to him, we could be devoured as was the Roman Empire.

In conclusion, I have tried my very best to describe my life, as well as those lives with whom I came in contact. Words, paper or time would not allow the numbers of names, friends and acquaintances I have enjoyed over these past sixty-five years.

From the supervisors who tried to slow me down in selling to the many pastors who have really tried to load my brain with God's Word and my old military buddies, both officer and enlisted, who supported me during my years of Military service, I am deeply indebted.

Even though the early years of my life were tough, and I did not think about them being tough then, the love within the family took the sting off and made life enjoyable. Remember, in the thirties and forties, everyone was in the same boat and really no one knew how bad things were.

I will always be indebted to my lovely wife who had to endure all these years with a traveling salesman. I can assure you one thing: I could not have achieved success in my life without this loving, reassuring wife. When I thought things were bad in every way, her ability to reassure me that it looked great on down the road worked. I could not have made it without her.

I am proud of my accomplishments, even though I don't put much stock in plaques, I am still proud to have received them from leadership and friends who I care much about.

*****

I would like to give credit to my parents for teaching me that Christ paid the ultimate price for my sins. They also taught me the rewards of being a person of integrity and commitment. I will always remember the switches mom made me cut to be used on me after I had been a naughty boy. All of them were needed and probably came short of others I should have had.

My brothers all taught me that love was the main ingredient in our family makeup and to never forget it. I have tried to pass this on to my wife, daughter, grandsons and their families. Love is a small four-letter word that is very strong. I give credit to my Lord who constantly gave it to us.

I am sure that I have left out many areas of my life that would have been meaningful in this book but, the memories that I have passed on in this book are truthful. I only wish that our young people would have to endure just enough hard times to find out the true meaning of family love. I have tried to portray the fact that you do not need money to be happy. Happiness in my life has been given me by trying to give to others.

Of course, just like anyone else, there are a few things that I would like to change, but not many. I count it many blessings for the many friends who I have made over the years, all over the world. I cannot imagine anyone not wanting friends.

My wife and I often talk about moving our home, giving away our assets that we have assembled over the years, and moving to a retirement home until we meet the Lord. I have told her many times that the only thing that would be wrong with it is we would not have our Sunday School friends whom we have known for years.

I jokingly said, "Nor would we have pall bearers for our funeral. We would have to hire some." There was no response from my lady.

I do wish I had mentioned more of my friends by name who have meant so much to me, but in so doing, I would leave someone out and hurt their feelings.

I do believe that Faith is needed in everyone's life to meet each day as it comes.

To believe in a future that is good is much better than looking for the bad in every day life and everyone you come in contact with. I have always been positive in my thoughts and actions. I, like many others, though, forget positives when things go bad, instead of looking on the bright side.

I have always said, "Take a sheet of paper, place at the top of one side, debits, and on top at the other side, place credits. Then list your debits and then your credits."

You will always find that the credits always exceed, by a large margin, your debits.

EPILOGUE
Honor Flights.com
A Pictoral View

Those of you who have not heard of "Honor Flights" should pay close attention to this writing.

When I was writing my book, "Brothers Four," I had not heard of "Honor Flights." I continued to write my book and when I was in the closing chapters, a wonderful friend and WWII veteran, David Murdoch, explained them to me.

David and about 149 other WWII vets and their "guardians" made this one-day visit to the WWII Memorial in Washington, D.C. Guardians were the persons that assisted the handicapped on the trip.

David did explain that Tyson Foods and Walmart, both of Northwest Arkansas, spent thousands of dollars twice a year to support these flights. At his insistence, I got on my computer, typed in "HonorFlights.com" and found a form to fill out to enable myself and others to make the trip. Little did I know what this trip would do for me and my life.

David, a fine Christian person and a member of the First Baptist Church in Russellville, served many combat positions in WWII and the Korean Conflict. David is a widower, after the passing of his wife, Jean, several years ago. He is an avid supporter of Veterans Day in Russellville and can always be seen either in the parade or waving an American flag on Main Street.

After this wonderful visit with David, I did pull up the application and there it was, asking for full information about my past service, etc. Of course, I served in WWII in the Pacific Combat area, which included time spent in New Guinea, the Philippines, and Australia, as well as service in the Korean conflict. My total service, active and reserve, was 37 years.

In filling out my application, memories danced through my mind about the deplorable conditions in New Guinea and the Philippines. I also thought of my many buddies that have gone on before me and had never had the opportunity to visit our Memorial.

In New Guinea, the natives had been brutally treated by the Japanese and we heard horror stories of the Japanese slipping into the tribal areas and raping and killing the natives. Since I was assigned to an Engineer Aviation Battalion, it was our assignment to clear the jungle with dozers and lay a mesh landing mat for the American fighters to land on.

You see, the jungle was really a rain forest and kept the jungle very wet and marshy. Many times, over the Guinea Bay, I have seen the Japanese Zeros shot down by our P-38 fighters. I never saw a P-38 downed by the Zeros. Of course, all of our engineers had our M-Garand rifles at ready in case we were attacked by enemy fire.

As you'd expect, it rained about 325 days a year in the jungles. We were all inoculated with many shots, including Typhus, Malaria, fevers of all kinds, as well as an Atabrin tablet each day for Malaria. We often saw rats the size of dachshund dogs run out of the Kuni grass.

My memories of Manila are more vivid than those of New Guinea. The living conditions were more tolerable. My recollections of the first sight of Manila was that of seeing leveled multi-storied buildings and children digging in American trash piles for food. We were very kind to these children. We often gave them our D bars (chocolate) and clothing.

Those years were hard ones and when the BIG Bad Bomb fell on Hiroshima, we all knew that home was not far away. There were sweet dreams from there on.

But enough about my service – now let us zero in on Honor Flights.

I finished my application, put a stamp on the envelope and mailed the application to the address specified. Many weeks rocked on and no answer came from my application. I began to wonder if there was a flight.

I was visiting with another WWII veteran here in Russellville a week or two later. This must have been in July or August 2011. He informed me that three of them had received their notices of the flight that was to leave Northwest Arkansas on October 15, 2011. I knew then that something was wrong and I began to check my computer and found that the Director of the Arkansas program was Bill McKenzie of Tyson Foods.

I tried calling him several times without luck. I happened to think of Senator Boozman's front man. I called him and he referred me to a wonderful lady by the name of Nancy Williams of Bella Vista, Arkansas. I called a number that was given me and a melodius voice at the other end of the line said, "This is Nancy Williams."

She asked me if I had mailed my application. I replied that I had. She replied that sometimes the applications got hung up at another site, so she said, "Let me check into it." About two days later, she called back and said that they had found my application and that I would be on the same flight with my friends. She was a wonderful, professional lady who loved assisting the veterans going on the flights that Tyson and Walmart provided.

There were four of us from the Russellville area that were selected to make the flight on October 15, 2011. These included: Winford Hoover, retired principal of schools, Jack Carpenter, retried businessman from Hamburg, Arkansas, Joe D. Bull, retired superintendent of schools from Hector, Arkansas, and myself.

Also, I need to note that a person that had for years spearheaded our Veteran's Day programs and parades in Russellville had mentioned to me that he would like to accompany his boys and the WWII ladies on this Honor Flight. Jim Bob Humphrey, owner of Humphrey Funeral Home, told me that he had always desired to be on one of these flights mainly because his dad was deceased and was a WWII veteran. I knew everyone would love to have Jim Bob on board, so I made another call.

I picked up the phone and called Mrs. Nancy Williams in Bella Vista, told her of my request for Jim Bob and what he had meant to all of the veterans in our area, and she responded, "Let me see what I can get done on this."

Later on that day, she called Jim Bob and told him that he was invited to make the trip to D.C. and serve as a Guardian. Jim Bob was thrilled to tears that he was going to make the trip he had longer for, for years. He handled the picture chores for us and could not keep up with the old WWII vets. Winford and I rode to NWA with Jim Bob and back home that evening. You should have heard all the war stories up there and back.

We checked into our motel, after a fine meal supplied by Jim Bob. So the excitement had just started and the day driving up before the flight the next day was great . . . now, what will happen from here on out?

Early the next day, we were up early showering, putting on our new shirts and caps depicting Honor Flights and finally getting ready for the BIG DAY. A short breakfast with plenty of anticipation, and we drove to NXA ready for departure. We parked the car, walked quite a distance to the boarding area, and were greeted by hundreds of people, some military, some school children and their teachers, all waving flags and shaking our hands and wishing us well on our one-day journey.

As we entered the clearance gate, Senator Boozman's rep and Congressman Womack's rep were there to shake our hands and wish us well, too. What a wonderful day this started off to be – but we weren't sure what awaited us in our nation's Capitol.

Before we get into the flight, I would like to extend additional information about my friend, Jim Bob Humphrey. For the past several years in Russellville, Jim Bob has taken it upon himself to organize and see to it that Russellville has the largest Veteran's Day parade in the state. I can tell you that it is phenomenal the way he gets all of our task force into the program and has a tremendous turnout each year on November 11th.

Huge numbers of floats, decorated banners, American flags, WWII Jeeps and, last year, of all things, he presented the people of our city with a Riderless Horse being escorted by field grade officers in their dress blues. Jim Bob has been influential in getting a fly-over of a military aircraft each year. Enough cannot be said about the hours and personal money that he spends in seeing that there is a top notch parade and program.

Another very important program that Jim Bob installed was a "Build a Bear" program, which was designed to see that each child of a deployed service person receives a talking bear from their parent. To date, more than 1,000 bears have been given at no cost to these children. These bears are expensive and there is a plan in the works to get large corporations to get involved in the funding of this program.

But, back to our exciting day. As we boarded the plane, there were three or four Tyson representatives there to greet us, shake our hands, and tell us what an honor it was to serve us on this one-day excursion. Of course, they were dressed in their khakis and we had a t-shirt and cap that addressed the day as Honor Flight. There was a lot of gray-haired men and women in wheelchairs or with walkers, crutches, and canes. But it did not matter because everyone was in wonderment about the day and the memories it would give them for a lifetime.

We were given a sack lunch to munch on as we flew toward D.C. It was a wonderful opportunity to sit with two good-looking people from Little Rock, Arkansas – a WWII veteran and his daughter. I had a wonderful time visiting with them on the flight.

As we taxied down the strip to take-off, there was a huge surge of water, a large spray that engulfed the entire airplane. I kew it was a clear day, so I wondered, "What was this spray?"

About that time, the Captain came on the intercom and said, "The spray is for dignitaries only, and I want you to know that you WWII vets fit the bill." He then told us to sit back and enjoy the flight.

In visiting with the veteran and his daughter from Little Rock, I happened to let them know that I had written a book, entitled "Brothers Four," and that the book concernment myself and my three brothers serving in WWII. I also mentioned that one of my deceased brothers' bombers, a B-26, was sitting in the Smithsonian and was named "Flak Bait."

We visited on about many things and soon the daughter asked, "Where could we buy one of your books?" I replied, "From me." After returning home, the daughter called and asked if

283

I had a supply of the books. I told her that I had them. The next day, she drove to Russellville and purchased two books. I enjoyed visiting with them very much and would like to visit again.

As we flew along, one of the Tyson attendants grabbed the microphone, asked if things were going well and added that it would be a short time when we would be landing. We prepared for landing and again anticipation began.

As our plane moved toward the gate, we were to pass under another large spray of water and we knew this time what that meant. The Captain announced that there were 150 dignitaries on the plane and they were treated thusly for their service. I had never considered myself a dignitary, but on this day I was finally receiving a "thank you" for my service to my country.

We pulled up to the gate, the door was opened and the WWII vets began disembarking. As I neared the door to reach the terminal, there was a huge noise as if there were several thousand bees. Well, as I stepped off the walkway, there must have been from 800 to 1,000 people there to meet us.

There were honor lines of active Military, Military Police, Guardsmen (all with their dress uniforms on) school teachers, their children, politicians from every state and people from every walk of life. They hugged us, thanked us for our service and greeted us in every way possible.

After we left this group, we were hustled back into a large round group, ready for instructions for the day. We were told which bus we would be going on and the number of the bus was on the front of the bus. We were finally going to get our chance to see our memorial.

When we boarded our bus, we were greeted by none other than Steve Womack, our Republican congressman from Rogers, Arkansas. The bus was silent as Mr. Womack spoke. He thanked us for our service and welcomed us to Washington. He passed out bottles of water and a brown sack of snacks. Mr. Womack stayed on our bus, even though we made all the stops at the memorials.

We travelled on our way to the WWII Memorial, and, as we travelled, a local lady on the bus pointed out many points of interest, with one of them being where the plane collided with the Pentagon on 9-11. She was a real sharp lady and made sure we were aware of all our great surroundings.

As we travelled on the bus, I could not help but think about my grandson, then Major but now Lt. Col. Cain Baker, and his family. With him were his wife, Courtney, and three little girls, Hannah, Caitlin, and Ashley, all awaiting my bus to spend time with me during my visit. Cain was currently stationed at the Pentagon.

As we approached the Memorial, there were demonstrators, carrying signs, etc. It took some time for the buses to get through this maze and get parked at the entrance of the Memorial. I could not believe what some of the signs read. It was my belief that the Memorial was hallowed ground and for a group of people to carry signs downing our Government hurt me a lot.

We finally made it. To see this massive structure, paid for by contributions from our WWII veterans, almost blew us away. As I stepped off the bus, my grandson, Cain, was the first to greet me and then his wife and little girls. It was so nice for he and his family to take the day and spend some of it with me. There were people from all over the United States and abroad there to view the Memorial and visit with our veterans.

I believe that the sight of the Memorial will always be thrust into my mind and heart. The fountains were massive, and the memorable plaques and carvings of the men and women that had sacrificed their lives for our right to enjoy freedom were so lifelike. Our men in wheelchairs, canes and walkers almost all had tears in their eyes. As we strolled, visited, took pictures and talked about the past, there was beautiful patriotic music being played softly.

My what a sight this was! It was also one that is difficult to explain to anyone. Veterans were standing under the engravings with the names of their home states while pictures were being snapped. This was an opportunity of a lifetime and no one wanted to waste one minute of their time. Our time was spent viewing, feeling and just enjoying this wonderful time with each other.

While I was viewing the Memorial, two young ladies approached me and said, "Sir, we want to thank you for your service, but would you mind sharing your combat experience during the war?" I thought for a moment and responded by telling them I served in the jungles of New Guinea and helped liberate Manila. I also served in the Korean Conflict. I related that the Japanese were still holding ground in New Guinea and, as Airborne Combat Engineers, we spent most of our time clearing the jungles and laying mesh for our fighters to land on . . . and, at the same time, we were expected to fight off the enemy.

I continued by sharing that we landed on Luzon and the Japanese were being pushed back by our forces and out of Manila. We visited on for quite awhile and they did mention their granddad was deceased and he had fought in the South Pacific also. There were at the Memorial to pay homage to their granddad and lived at that time in California.

Finally, it was time to visit with Senator Bob Dole, a WWII veteran, and his wife. They had made nearly all of the trips of veterans to the Memorial and spent time signing autographs and relaying messages about his service during the war. I will never forget how many persons crowded around the Senator and his wife. Everyone wanted to get their picture made with him, of course. This says a lot about veterans taking care of veterans. Even with his wounds during WWII, he thought enough of his comrades to come thousands of miles to be with them. I understood that he and his wife, up to our flight, had met all the flights. It was quite an experience to be near a decorated WWII veteran who had also gone on to serve his country as a Senator.

After bidding farewell to my grandson and his family, we started toward the bus. But we were stopped by a Tyson Foods' photographer who asked if he could get some footage of my family as a testimonial. It was to be used for future Honor Flights. My grandson, Cain, his eldest daughter, Hannah, and I posed and spoke about the wonderful trip that Tyson had provided. This was wonderful for me since I had spent over fifty years working with Tyson people in the poultry industry and was a friend of Don Tyson and his son, Johnny.

Upon entering the buses, we were told we would visit all the Memorials. Those of you who have visited Washington before know how many memorials there are, so we began to get on and off the buses at each Memorial, listening to a quick earful from a guide, before heading on to the next Memorial.

Again, we were so fortunate to have wonderful guides. Of course, the Korean

Memorial was so lifelike and the wall was a sight to see. I did want to see the WWI Memorial dedicated to people like my dad, who served in France. He fought in the Argonne Forest and was wounded. The wounds finally led to his early death at age 38. But when we were in D.C., the Memorial was under repair and no one was allowed to view it.

I believe the Air Force Memorial was the last on our tour, so after that viewing, we boarded the buses and were back on our way to the terminal to fly back to Northwest Arkansas.

As we walked into the terminal, I could hear loud music and loud clapping and laughing. As I walked down the hall, I could see a group of WWII veterans and middle-aged ladies jitterbugging to music from the 1940s and '50s. There was an excellent band trumpeting out tunes from Glenn Miller and Artie Shaw, and many veterans dancing with the young ladies that were there to provide partners. Let me tell you – these guys still had the moves and the desire. This was a very nice gesture on the part of Tyson and Walmart.

As we sat and waited to board our plane, we enjoyed visiting with other veterans, both male and female. We were all tired and anxious to get home, though, and the day was quickly coming to an end. We were finally called to board the aircraft. We lined up and awaited our turn to go through the door and to our assigned seat.

All of a sudden, I noticed a very nice looking young lady putting on lipstick and standing at the door of the plane. As each veteran entered the door, this lady kissed each one on the cheek. Oh yes, I had the opportunity to get smacked on the cheek. When I returned home that evening and told my wife about the kiss, she remarked, "I don't suppose you will shower for at least a month?"

We were all seated and our Tyson Guides began making statements about our return flight to Arkansas. They thanked us again for being good and being on time and also, again, for our service. As we taxied out to the runway to take off, there was another spray of water on our plane to signify dignitary status for all of us. We again gave the whole crew a big hand for a nice day in D.C. And then we were off and into the air.

As we took off and were levelling off, thoughts raced through my head of my prior service and what this day had meant to me and

291

my buddies. We all knew there would be a lot of loved ones there at the airport to greet our return, and there was excitement to get back and share our memories with the rest of our friends and family.

We continued to eat out of our sack lunches and visit with each other. As we neared the airport, all of the Tyson staff came on the intercom to express their appreciation for all of our activities on the day and, again, for our service. The pilot came on the intercom and said that we would be landing shortly. As we touched down, no one could have imagined what was awaiting us inside the airport.

But, even before we got inside, one of the most inspiring and enthusing parts of our trip was when we were taxiing to the gate and the Command Pilot came on the intercom. He shared these comments: "I would like to sincerely thank each of you for flying with us today and thank you for your valuable service to your country. This was my 125th flight with Honor Flights and I look forward to many more. It is my hope that each of you will have a continued lengthy life and one filled with joy and happiness." Everyone on the plane gave the pilot a big hand as we pulled up to the gate.

Each Tyson staff member shook each hand of the veterans and wished them well in the future as we disembarked. As we walked down the long hall to the entrance of the airport, you could hear music and a humming effect as though there were bees nearby. As we entered the large terminal, there was a greeting line of about 500 or more people. Again, many of them were teachers with their students, as well as more family members, and they were all clapping, shaking hands, and thanking us for our service. Over in one corner was a men's choir perfoming patriotic songs, and it was some of the most beautiful music possible for a gathering such as this.

Winford Hoover, one of my buddies, was following us and I said, "Win, let's get us a crowd of these little students and give them a great, big hug." The families and teachers were taking pictures, so there were many photos taken of us and everyone else there.

Can you believe these young ones, chaperoned by their teachers, stayed up until 9 or 10 P.M. to welcome us back home? It was fantastic.

But that wasn't all. Each child handed us a pack of letters that they and their classmates had written. I suppose each vet had over ten packs of letters from school children from schools all over Northwest Arkansas. This was such a joyous occasion that we just wanted to hang around and visit, but we were rushed by Jim Bob Humphrey, our driver, to our car and headed home.

We thoroughly enjoyed our trip home from NXA as much as we enjoyed driving up. We spent much time rehashing the day in D.C. Jim Bob was overjoyed at being invited as a Guardian. Jim Bob did remark, however, that all the "old" vets had worn him out. We can't appreciate Jim Bob enough for what he has done and will be doing for our veterans in the future.

When we had our planning meeting for the next Veteran's Day Parade, Jim Bob had over 300 pictures displayed on his big screen depicting our trip to D.C. Everyone there, probably fifteen folks, asked many questions about the trip and Jim Bob was glad to answer all of them.

After my great experience, I became very aware of other veterans who would qualify for the unique experience of the Honor Flight. One such friend was Gordon Trusty, a resident of

Midway, Arkansas. Just recently, he and his son, Danny Trusty, made the flight.

Danny's wife, Carol, was employed by Arkansas Tech University with years of honorable service before her retirement, and she was the strong arm in connecting her family with Honor Flight.

One day, I had asked Carol if her father-in-law, Gordon, had ever been on Honor Flight. I knew he was an aging WWII veteran, too. She indicated that he hadn't made the trip and I asked her to get a form, fill it out, and have him sign it so we could see what could be done. She loved the idea and filled out the form and mailed it. She indicated that Danny would accompany him on the trip.

Well, a few weeks passed and she called one day and said she had not heard a thing. Again, I called Nancy Williams of Bella Vista, gave her the details, and, just like that, he was approved. Carol was willing to pay her way just to be there with Danny and Gordon, but the plan failed and she did not get to go. Here are just a few of their statements when they returned:

Danny remarked, "I have never witnessed anything like this in my life. To see so many veterans, tears in their eyes, and hear their remarks, will always ring in my ears. There is no doubt that this trip was one of the high marks of my life."

Gordon said, "This one trip I will never forget. How can I ever thank Tyson and Walmart and all their people that made this so wonderful? My daughter-in-law was responsible for getting Danny and I aboard, and I think her so much for the time she spent."

I might mention that Gordon Trusty is a widower that lives alone in rural Logan County. After retiring from Civil Service many years ago, Gordon busied himself by making a huge garden every year and selling his produce at a Farmers Market in Russellville twice a week. This past spring and summer, I visited Gordon's tent at the Market.

Everyone loves Gordon and enjoys being his friend. He is a man of faith, a Christian, and he loves people. Even though he is in his 90's, no one dares to try and stay up with him in his daily chores. He is a dedicated father and someone we would all like to pattern our lives after. I am proud to have had a small part in positioning Gordon and Danny to make this wonderful trip.

Final Thanks

Within this epilogue, I would be remiss if I did not offer two special thank you's. First of all, the Russellville High School gave us a great celebration recently for Veteran's Day.

The two great leaders of this program were Mrs. Jacobs and Mrs. Stobaugh. These ladies put together a program that rivalled Jim Bob's great Veteran's Day parade.

The whole student body was present for the activities that lasted over an hour and half. I must say that I have never witnessed a group of students, especially of that size and numbers, behave themselves in such an orderly and quiet manner, listening to every word said during the program. I was honored to speak during the program about my service during WWII and the Korean Conflict, and I got to wear my dress blue uniform. The other speaker was Congressman Tom Cotton, a Dardanelle native.

As I wrote the Superintendent of Schools, Mr. Randall Williams, "I have never witnessed a program as huge in numbers, and I must say that Mrs. Jacobs and Mrs. Stobaugh spent many hours preparing and presenting this outstanding program." I also wrote, "You should be proud to have persons of this leadership ability that are so gracious in their acts of leadership."

I would like to mention Colonel Joy Leapheart, President of the MOAA chapter in Russellville, who contributed to the preparation of the program that day. After visiting with the ladies after the program, it was decided that this would be an ongoing affair each year to recognize those individuals that gave so much to their country.

Finally, I would like to finish by listing all those friends and loved ones that enjoyed the sights and sounds of that day we spent at the WWII Memorial in Washington, D.C.

I will try to remember those that I knew from this area that attended. Those are: David Murdoch, Karen Yarborough (guide), Arnold Bowden (guide), Harvey Young, Troy Burris, Charles Wesley, Scrappy Smith, Joe D. Bull, Winford Hoover, Jack Carpenter, and many others that I know that refused to fly.

I must also thank the Tyson staff that assisted us at each venue and the Congressional group that either met our flight or spent the time at the Memorial with us. And the many thousands of people that saw us off at NXA airport in

Springdale, the ones that met us at the airport in D.C., and the great crowd, including teachers, students, and military, thta met us when our plane landed back in NXA.

When you are in your nineties and you still have your memory and the ability to move around and visit with those in WWII, you can say, "Job well done, good and faithful servant." I would just like to say that this day is one that will be remembered by all in attendance.

I would also like to thank one of the strongest arms of these flights for taking the time to get involved because of her heart to see all these WWII vets enjoy the day of their lives. This person's name, of course, is Nancy Williams. She lives in Bella Vista and, I can tell you for sure, SHE GETS THE JOB DONE. Thanks so much, Nancy, and we will always remember you and how you gave you last ounce of energy to see that each veteran had the opportunity to see their Memorial.

Writing this epilogue has been a lot of fun and the memories it brought back are enormous in my life.

Above: WWII Memorial with fountains
Below: Jock with the BakerFamily at the Memorial

Left: Winfred Hoover with Jock and Hannah Baker

Below: Vets waiting to board the flight back home

<u>*Above:*</u> *Plenty of kisses for the vets boarding the plane*
<u>*Below:*</u> *Ginger and Nan with their dad*

<u>Above:</u> (Left to right) Joe D. Bull, Jock, Hoover and their guide
<u>Below:</u> Rep. Steve Womack with veteran

<u>Above:</u>
David
Murdoch
surrounded
by military

<u>Left:</u> David
Murdoch in
WWII
uniform

304

Above: Senator and Mrs. Bob Dole meet veterans
Below: Everyone aboard – on to D. C.

Above: Senator John Boozman boards plane to welcome the veterans
Below: Hundreds of happy faces

Above: (Left to right) Gordon and Danny Trusty
Below: ALL ABOARD VETERANS

Left: Gordon Trusty at his best

On the final pages, you will see the following images:
1. *Letter of appreciation from Congressman Steve Womack*
2. *Letter of appreciation from Donnie Smith, President and CEO of Tyson Foods, Inc.*
3. *Program, Russellville High School Veterans' Day 2013 observance*

Congress of the United States
House of Representatives
Washington, DC 20515–0403

October 15, 2011

Dear Honored Veteran:

I am pleased to welcome you to Washington, D.C. for your visit to the World War II Memorial. What an honor it is for me, personally, to be part of this event.

I am always honored to be in the presence of men and women who have served their country in uniform—and specifically, those who represent America's Greatest Generation. I often quote from Tom Brokaw's book when speaking in patriotic ceremonies. To know that each of you played an important part in the effort that "…won the war and saved the world…" is an inspiration to me.

Our Country owes you a debt of gratitude that can never be repaid.

I would like to thank Tyson Foods and Wal-Mart for sponsoring this event. I also thank Bill McKenzie of Tyson Foods for his personal involvement. It speaks well of a nation when its people honor the service of its veterans.

I look forward to our time together and trust that the visit to your memorial will be one of the highlights of your life. Thank you for your service to this great Nation.

See you in Washington, D.C.!

Steve Womack
Member of Congress

WASHINGTON DC
1508 LONGWORTH HOUSE OFFICE BUILDING
WASHINGTON, DC 20515
(202) 225-4301

ROGERS
3333 PINNACLE HILLS PARKWAY, #120
ROGERS, AR 72758
(479) 464-0446

FORT SMITH
423 NORTH 6TH STREET
FORT SMITH, AR 72902
(479) 424-1146

HARRISON
303 NORTH MAIN STREET, SUITE 102
HARRISON, AR 72601
(870) 741-6900

PRINTED ON RECYCLED PAPER

309

October 15, 2011

Dear Honor Flight Veteran,

On behalf of the more than 96,000 people who work for Tyson Foods in the United States, I extend my appreciation to you for your service to our country. We consider it a privilege for Tyson to help support and coordinate this special Honor Flight trip and are pleased you have the opportunity to see the memorial dedicated in your honor.

As you reflect on this day and your visit to the memorial that recognizes those who served in World War II, we hope you feel the same pride that so many of us have for veterans like you.

When you left home during World War II, it must have been very difficult to leave your family and friends behind. Yet, you were willing to leave the safety and comfort of the familiar in order to serve your country and protect the ones you loved. Because of you and your fellow veterans, today we have the freedoms we all enjoy here in the United States. Words are not enough to express our gratitude.

Thank you,

Donnie Smith
President and CEO
Tyson Foods, Inc.

2200 Don Tyson Parkway • SPRINGDALE, ARKANSAS 72762-6999 •
(479) 290 4617 Fax (479) 757-6772 • email donnie.smith@tyson.com

Program Order of Events

Welcome by Sheila Jacobs

Presentation of the flags by Honor Guard

Pledge of Allegiance by Marco Monterrosa

National Anthem performed by RHS Band Trumpets

Congressman Tom Cotton introduced by Mrs. Sarah Stobaugh

Blades of Grass and Pure White Stones, Arranged by Keith Christopher and performed by the RHS Choir

Major Jock Davis introduced by Mrs. Sarah Stobaugh

Presentation of Interact Wall of Honor Awards

- Corporal Gene Riggs

    United States Army

- Lawrence Vernon

    Airman Second Class

    United States Air Force

- Sergeant Major Raymond Daniel Pardue

    United States Army

Salute to the Armed Forces, Arranged by Camp Kirkland and performed by the RHS Choir

Closing Remarks by Sheila Jacobs

Congressman Tom Cotton

Tom Cotton is a sixth generation Arkansan who was born and raised on his family's cattle farm in Yell County. After attending Dardanelle High School, Tom went on to graduate from Harvard and Harvard Law School.

The tragic attacks of September 11, 2001 occurred during Tom's final year of law school, and he began to reconsider his future plans. He ultimately left law after clerking for the U.S. Court of Appeals and short time in a private law practice to join the United States Army. Tom declined a commission as a JAG attorney and opted to serve as an infantry officer.

Tom Cotton served almost five years as an active duty infantry officer and completed combat tours in both Iraq and Afghanistan. In Iraq, Tom served with the 101st Airborne where he led an infantry platoon in daily combat patrols. While in Afghanistan, he served as the operations officer for a Provincial Reconstruction Team. Between his two combat tours, he served as a platoon leader with the Old Guard at Arlington National Cemetery, the unit responsible for military honors funerals. Tom's military decorations include the Bronze Star Medal, Combat Infantry Badge, and Ranger Tab.

After leaving active duty, Tom worked as a management consultant for McKinsey & Co. He represents Arkansas's fourth district in the United States House of Representatives.

Major Jock Davis

Jock Davis was born in Malvern, Arkansas on Oct. 12, 1924. At an early age he and his family moved to Prescott, Arkansas. After graduation, he entered the Army and served two and a half years in combat areas of New Guinea and the Philippines. Upon his honorable discharge and coming home, Jock entered Arkansas Tech and graduated four years later with a B.S. Degree in Business. Jock has served on the Arkansas Tech University Alumni Association, by serving as President for two terms and was active on its board for about 20 years. He has been elected to Tech's Hall of Distinction, which is the highest honor given an alumni.

Jock has served for many volunteer organizations in the city of Russellville, most notably as President of the Russellville Jaycees. He helped guide this organization to many national honors. His professional career spanned over 50 years serving Agriculture Business in sales and was named the number one sales person out of 350 salesmen that spanned the United States.

Jock served 37 years in active and reserve service retiring as a Major. He is proud of his heritage in the military; his dad served in WWI; his son-in-law is a retired Lt. Col., Army, and he has three grandsons that fought in the Iraq and Afghanistan areas for eleven trips abroad. Among them there are two Apache Pilots and the other a Company Commander, Infantry. There ranks are Lt. Col., Major and Captain. Jock and his wife, Melba have one daughter, "Jibby", a graduate of Russellville High and Ouachita Baptist University and has retired from teaching in Georgia after thirty two years in the profession.

Made in the USA
Middletown, DE
30 October 2023